PEOPLE AND STORIES / GENTE Y CUENTOS

PEOPLE AND STORIES / GENTE Y CUENTOS

WHO OWNS LITERATURE?
COMMUNITIES FIND THEIR VOICE
THROUGH SHORT STORIES

SARAH HIRSCHMAN

iUniverse, Inc.
NEW YORK   BLOOMINGTON

PEOPLE AND STORIES / GENTE Y CUENTOS
Who Owns Literature? Communities Find
Their Voice Through Short Stories

iUniverse books may be ordered through booksellers or by contacting:

iUniverse
1663 Liberty Drive
Bloomington, IN 47403
www.iuniverse.com
1-800-Authors (1-800-288-4677)

Because of the dynamic nature of the Internet, any Web addresses or links contained in this book may have changed since publication and may no longer be valid.

ISBN: 978-1-4401-8698-1 (sc)
ISBN: 978-1-4401-8700-1 (dj)
ISBN: 978-1-4401-8699-8 (ebk)

Printed in the United States of America

iUniverse rev. date: 12/8/2009

For Katia

CONTENTS

ACKNOWLEDGEMENTS

My desire to write this book was first brought about by my wish to share the excitement that I often experienced during People and Stories/Gente y Cuentos sessions that I coordinated; I wanted to tell others about how people who rarely read could become so engaged in conversations about literary short stories; I wanted to recapture those voices, their new self assertiveness, their pride at being able to take part in a common cultural good. The detailed examples throughout the book are there to transmit the liveliness of these dialogues. Moreover, to answer the questions of those who often doubt that such complex, literary texts can be understood by such unprepared readers, I describe the method I developed over a period of years to help that process and the influences which led me on that path.

In *Origins*, I describe the various literary theories and personal experiences that brought me to contemplate the possibility of interweaving perceptions of common people with complex texts of literature. I trace how I came to believe that it would be possible for them to draw upon their life experience to enter the short story and respond to the images, shadows, poetic surprises of a text. In the chapter *The Actors*, I share the method which I developed to make this happen in community settings. Details are spelled out on how such meetings can be organized, how short stories are to be prepared for discussions, how questions can be formulated, how coordinators are to ready themselves for the sessions. This description of "how we do it" will hopefully motivate others to contact us to help organize similar groups in their communities.

During the first ten years of this endeavor, as I worked alone experimenting with different approaches, my late daughter Lisa, a clinical psychologist, helped me with well placed energetic thrusts—she just would not let me give up; it is with her tender and wise help, that I was able to surmount recurring moments of discouragement. My husband Albert was a willing and careful reader of the short stories in Spanish as I was building up my first bibliography. His writings on economic development and his observations on the various, often unexpected ways that growth occurs, gave me the necessary trust in the power of people's imagination. More recently, my Parisian daughter Katia has become indispensable. Her writing and organizational skills as well as her enthusiasm for this endeavor have made her loving help invaluable to me. Besides helping in the production of this book, she now has developed a French version of the program both in a prison outside of Paris and in rural areas in the south west of France.

Pat Andres, who is today the Executive Director of the People and Stories/Gente y Cuentos program, has been an interlocutor for more than twenty years, first as coordinator, then as co-director, and finally as director. Her energy and tireless enthusiasm for the project have given it new dimensions. She has imaginatively experimented with new groups, trained coordinators, and has developed broad support for our work. The growth and vigor of today's program is in great part due to her leadership.

This book has been inspired by my work with the People and Stories/Gente y Cuentos programs and these could not have existed without the help of so many generous friends and Foundations. I am also grateful to our dynamic Board whose members have supported and encouraged the publication of this book.

I also owe much to conversations with colleagues and friends, too numerous to list here; friends who have suggested titles of stories, new approaches, or simply encouraged me in this project— Geneviève Patte, Jim Irby, Ricardo Piglia, María del Carmen Feijoó, Beatriz Sarlo, Ariel Dorfman, Roberto Schwarz, Ruth Cardoso, Judy Hemschemeyer, Joseph Frank, Arcadio Díaz, Joan Scott, Rebecca Scott, C.K.Williams. Peter Jaszi and his students have helped with some expert legal advice. And over the years close literary work with Marcy Schwartz, Lawrence McCarty, and Alma Concepción has helped me to approach texts in interesting new ways.

The friendship of Hildred Geertz has supported me all along the writing of this book and her critical mind has time and again sharpened my thinking. She, as well as Danielle Allen, have read the manuscript and contributed detailed and helpful comments. Jim Clark has helped generously with expert guidance related to the publishing of this volume.

My greatest gratitude goes to the many, many women, men, adolescents both in this country and in Latin America who joined me with so much gusto in discussing stories, sharing memories, comparing perceptions—I have learned much from them.

PREFACE

In the twenty-first century, how a country educates will decide its prospects for advancing the cause of social justice within its borders. We now commonly hear politicians and policy-makers touting the need for a well-educated populace to compete in the world's permanently globalized and currently knowledge-based economy. Their speeches conjure up images not of the grimy industrial armies of the past but of gleaming squads of tech-savvy inventors, innovators, and creators. Yet in these visions, the new bright squads, like their coal-blackened predecessors, have primarily the job of filling the national coffers. Only infrequently do we hear a politician discuss education in terms of any given individual's potential for flourishing. Rarely do we hear the hope that an education, appropriately conceived, might first and foremost break down social alienation and isolation, empower the disempowered, or strengthen the egalitarian basis of democratic life. Sarah Hirschman's book is officially part memoir and part pedagogic manual, but it is really a manifesto for an approach to education that does all these more human, more important things.

In 1969, Hirschman attended a seminar at Harvard with Paulo Freire, a Brazilian philosopher and educator, who developed literacy programs with the goal of consciousness-raising. Consciousness-raising occurs, Hirschman writes, "as people deepen their understanding of their condition and attempt to improve their control over it." Such learning supplants "what Freire contemptuously dismissed as 'banking education' where teachers deposit new information which they deem important into the minds of accepting, passive students." Freire's literacy programs focused on generating dialogue among disempowered, alienated, often impoverished students; dialogues would be launched by projecting on the wall a picture of something of immediate concern to the participants: a well, for instance, in places where debates about water rights and land ownership were intense. Hirschman wondered whether "varied, richly, textured literary works," and in particular short stories, could have the same liberating, empowering effect—whether a mode of education based on literary story discussions could lead to measurable improvements in quality of life for the disadvantaged.

She started her program, Gente y Cuentos ("People and Stories") in 1972 in a low-income housing project in Cambridge, MA, with an informal invitation to participate addressed to a group of young Latina women sitting on their stoops minding their children. From then until the present, Hirschman has worked steadily on improving and institutionalizing her program. English sessions were added in 1986, and People and Stories/Gente y Cuentos, as it is now called, has since become a formal non-profit organization with programs in over fourteen US states, Latin America, and France. Hirschman reviews the development of the program and, in her book's most valuable contribution, sets out the pedagogic methods, refined over time that can successfully generate the liberating dialogue she, like Freire, sought. While Hirschman's educational program recruits primarily from disempowered and disadvantaged adult populations, her clear account of precisely how and why engaging with the rich and varied texture of good short stories can jumpstart the internal and independent evolution of consciousness in people is worth reading for any teacher, regardless of their students' backgrounds. Hirschman reminds us of what we are trying to do when we introduce any person to literature and, remarkably, she explains why it works. This is a rare achievement.

When Hirschman began her enterprise, she was of course warned away from using "high literature" for programs for the disadvantaged. Some of her fellow Freire students "objected to the use of works of fiction as both too remote and too complex for groups whose concerns appear removed from literature." Her academic friends charged her with being both utopian and populist, asking: "How could uneducated minds who had not read much understand and discuss sophisticated writers?" The value of Hirschman's program for a social justice initiative lies just here, in her resistance to these objections. Her book is wonderfully embroidered with anecdotes of, as she puts it, "the disparate, small dramatic happenings that took place during the different sessions." These happenings consist over and over again of the falling of psychological barriers that had stood in the way of personal empowerment. Among the multiple barriers that fall is also the very simple one inherent in the idea that there are some things that just belong to elites and not to anyone else.

Speaking of "Tuesday Siesta" by Gabriel García Márquez, Hirschman writes: "The story emerges through a series of confrontations in which we become emotionally involved, partly because each of us has lived through conflicts somewhat similar to these and partly because the clashes in the story are taking hold of us." Note her use of "we." Hirschman's argument is fundamentally egalitarian: her account of why literature might raise the consciousness of the participants in Gente y Cuentos is the same as her account of why it might raise her own. And, as you might imagine, Hirschman's educational background is pretty elite. As the participants in Gente y Cuentos transform stories by elite authors into the instruments of their own learning and self-development, they also demystify social hierarchy and reclaim the basic truth of human equality. Hirschman's account beautifully captures a pedagogic approach that would indeed plant empowerment, and so social justice, at the heart of an educational system.

Danielle Allen, Professor
Institute for Advanced Study
Princeton, NJ
August 2009

INTRODUCTION

Each of us may be curious about the other in our multicultural, multiclass society but it is difficult to talk to strangers. It is even more difficult for our educators to find ways to engage and motivate voices and to establish a common ground with people that are so different from each other and where so many have been denied an orderly and complete education. Yet as democratic citizens, we have established laudable goals as expressed in Article twenty seven of the Universal Declaration of Human Rights of 1948 which states "Everyone has the right freely to participate in the cultural life of the community, to enjoy the arts and to share in scientific advancement and its benefits." But what exactly are we doing to translate these goals on the ground?

People and Stories/Gente y Cuentos is a venture which is a small personal attempt to realize in the real world of our communities some of our lofty declarations of principle. In the pages that follow, I propose to share the excitement of my own discovery that literature, which is usually seen as reserved for the few, can become the arena where unusual connections are established among people who ordinarily have no access to it. People find their own voice and a new self-assurance as the fictional text helps develop a surprising ability to manipulate ideas as well as share with each other personal feelings.

In a first chapter, **ENCOUNTERS THROUGH LITERATURE,** I describe the search for new ways to bring literature and ordinary people to interact. To set the scene, **An Unusual Meeting** lets the reader observe a real encounter in Trenton, NJ. **Stories and Story Telling -- A Tradition**, gives some background information on the participants. **The Challenge of Adult Education** answers those who claim that there are faster, more direct ways to educate.

A second chapter, **ORIGINS** traces the various influences that brought me to structure People and Stories/Gente y Cuentos. The importance of the ideas of **Paulo Freire,** a Brazilian philosopher and educator, is followed by **Other Thinkers** who have searched for round about ways to reach certain goals. Finally **New Reader Response** discusses some of the philosophers and literary critics who helped me to develop my own method. This chapter concludes with **A New Venture**, the actual launch of the first experimental session.

The third chapter, **THE ACTORS: STORIES, COORDINA-TORS, GROUPS** sets out in detail what it takes to make such an approach successful. The critical work that has to be done on the story and the preparation of questions are described in **Stories** and **Coordinators.** The following section entitled **Groups,** with its examples of different group configurations, offers a number of detailed vignettes of how discussions developed during actual sessions in New Jersey and in Argentina.

The two last sections, **UNDERSTANDING THE OTHER THROUGH LITERATURE** and **THE ROAD TRAVELED,** evoke the sometimes unexpected benefits of the approach set out in People and Stories/Gente y Cuentos. Finally, the appendices provide practical details for those interested in going further.

I hope that this personal recounting of my quest to reach others will be useful both to people interested in the influence that fiction can have on our lives and to educators searching for ways to develop new methods to respond to the needs of the various groups that make up our contemporary society.

ENCOUNTERS THROUGH LITERATURE

AN UNUSUAL MEETING

"Ah, a rainbow is always good news: When the Lord wanted to let Noah know that the flood was over, that the flood would not return, He sent a rainbow over the clouds," said Pedro, a Puerto Rican man, one night, in the basement of a church in Trenton, New Jersey. A short story by Arguedas, the Peruvian writer, had just been read aloud in Spanish to a group from the local Latino[1] community. In it a shepherd clutching his beloved dog flees from a burning hacienda; he trusts that somehow, way

---

1　　No single term can designate adequately the various Spanish-speaking groups we are addressing in Gente y Cuentos (GyC). In Eastern United States, Puerto Ricans as well as many Latin Americans refer to themselves as Hispanos/as, while the Mexican Americans of the Southwest and of the West prefer Chicanos/as or La Raza. Others use terms such as Latino, Latin American, Hispano American. Our use of Hispanic or Latino will have to serve as an approximate and general short-cut designation for a number of different groups that are located in the United States but see themselves as culturally related to areas of Latin America, the Caribbean, or Mexico.

up in the highlands, he'll find a place to work; if not, he can always go higher, up the rainbow, to God who will take care of him and his dog.

Pedro had responded to the announcement of a new type of gathering to be held once a week in the rooms of a Catholic church where Sunday mass was celebrated in the Spanish language. "Everyone is welcome," said the recruiting notice, "you need only know Spanish to enroll." The man who recalled the rainbow as the Lord's sign to Noah had never before joined the discussion. Pedro was shy, inhibited, embarrassed about not being able to read, but now he spoke up. Something in the Peruvian story struck a responsive chord in him. Others in the group, somewhat more educated, were startled by the evocative quality of his remarks. Pedro spoke more often after that night.

The kind of comments that the Arguedas' story generated are often heard during People and Stories/Gente y Cuentos sessions, a program which organizes readings and discussions of short stories with persons who have never had access to literature. Trust in the power of literature to open up to different readings, and trust in the ability of persons to draw on their life experience to enter the world of fiction, have been at the root of this enterprise.

Gente y Cuentos held in Spanish started informally as a weekly affair. People came not only to hear and discuss stories but also to find companionship with others who spoke Spanish. Soon, the success of the program brought the local community college, which was designing a new inner-city curriculum, to sponsor the sessions. "Graduation" was celebrated with a distribution of certificates, food cooked by the participants, and even dancing to the sound of salsa. The local paper printed a story with unusual photos: urban Latino dwellers sitting around a table in animated discussion of a short story written by one of their authors. Some participants became more self-confident and began to wander over to a High School Equivalency program (GED) given elsewhere in town and to inquire about new English-as-a-Second-Language (ESL) courses.

People and Stories/Gente y Cuentos was born.

After more than thirty five years of experience with the program, I want to revisit its beginnings, describe its growth, and take stock of the outcomes.

How did this unlikely enterprise take place at all? How could complex short stories be read and discussed by a group of adults whose education did not prepare them for so demanding a task? Could this activity which at first only wanted to bring a new group of readers to enjoy literature result indirectly in an innovative approach to what we call education?

STORIES AND STORY TELLING – A TRADITION

The power of stories is perhaps most strikingly illustrated by the extraordinary feat of Scheherazade, the legendary Persian maiden who managed to survive by keeping a cruel king on tenterhooks through her one thousand and one suspense tales. Among other examples, one can cite the "veillées" of early peasant France where after the evening meal, as darkness descended on the village, folks crowded together to keep warm and tell stories which entertained and bound members of a household. In another setting, in nineteenth century Cuba, tobacco workers enjoyed being read to in cigar factories. When some of them emigrated to Florida towards the end of the century, they established this custom there. A "lector" (reader), paid voluntarily by the workers, was asked to read in a clear and strong voice (sometimes to as many as four hundred workers!) and with "feeling" both news items and installments of novels and plays—Pérez Galdós, Zola, Cervantes, Molière. Later, during some strikes, the continued presence of lectors, who were often disliked by the company, became one of the workers' insistent demands; but eventually, the management won out and the readings were finally altogether forbidden.[2]

Popular culture is full of forms related to literature: proverbs, fairy tales, cherished verses, ballads, and spirituals. The Bible and other sacred texts, which many community adults know so much better than college students, serve as a rich introduction to literary works. Most people are accustomed to tolerate ambiguous expressions and enjoy disguised meanings. The taste for expressive rhythms, sound effects, or repetitions is universal. The sheer joy that emanates from a group singing couplets at a fiesta to the accompaniment of a guitar, the laughter that greets the punch line of a good joke-teller, the enthusiasm of children repeating some fairy tale magic formula, the rhythmic responses of an African American audience in church or at a play, attest to the relish with which people savor their own language. The pleasure becomes even more exciting as various members of the public freely add embellishments and variations and begin to hear their own active voices as part of an emergent dialogue. The deft manipulation of one's own language is not only a source of pleasure—it is also a source of power. Street language, for example, can violate grammar rules and can be at times jarring, but it is often effective and innovative. In fact, many writers, Gogol, Flaubert, Flannery O'Connor, and so many others, have been known to spend much time listening and carefully noting expressions heard in public places. Much of the literature that is

2   Sir Richard Francis Burton. *The Thousand Nights and a Night.* London, H.S. Nichols & Co. 1885-88. Emilie Carles. *Une soupe aux herbes sauvages.* Jean-Claude Simoen, 1977, pp.28-31. Louis A. Perez. *Cuban History.* University Press of Florida, 1995, pp.73-78. Fernando Ortiz, *Cuban Counterpoint.* Duke University Press, 1995, pp.89-92.

supposed to be so remote from the uneducated people is partly built with elements that they themselves have furnished.

Those objecting to my approach sometimes claim that the rapport with one's own language and popular culture comes naturally; it's been there since childhood. To embark on a discussion of an unfamiliar work of fiction or poetry is quite another matter. In any event, literature is often distrusted for a variety of contradictory reasons: sometimes it is seen as too forbidding and too arduous; sometimes, on the contrary, it is dismissed as merely pleasing, or too trivial to compete with "really useful" pursuits; would it not be better to spend the precious time that working people can devote to improve their education with a more conventional Adult Education program?

THE CHALLENGE OF ADULT EDUCATION

Efforts have been made to help the many people who, for one reason or another, have not been able to finish their education— high school dropouts, immigrants, struggling adults of all ages who look for another chance. Since the time in 1972 when I began to organize Gente y Cuentos, those programs have been much improved. New research by scholars at various places and notably at the Harvard Graduate School of Education[3] has improved the manner to recruit and motivate students, to understand their needs and to adjust the curriculum. But the challenge remains: adults come to these programs late in life with a variety of past experiences and uneven knowledge; they also often suffer from a lack of self confidence partly due to bad experiences that they have had in the past in school or at work. Rather than grapple with

---

3   Also: National Center for Study of Adult Learning and Literacy (NCSALL). Boston, MA.

what appears as an inchoate and inapplicable past experience, some states and the federal government have set up a number of training programs to prepare people for a productive life of work in the United States. Courses in English-as-a-Second-Language (ESL) and in literacy have been developed; training and examinations for a high school equivalency certificate (G.E.D.) are offered and financial help is available for those who want to prepare for these tests. Other centers specialize in skill-training with batteries of supportive basic courses in ESL, reading, arithmetic. All these programs operate along the same general lines: the incoming individuals are tested and their level is established. After this a training program is charted to launch them on a successful career in the world of work. But the going is far from smooth.

Appropriate testing of individuals is a difficult art. Persons from other cultures may misinterpret questions and teenagers in difficulty may be too discouraged to perform under stress. Most training and basic education programs are limited to measuring how well students can manipulate "basic" academic subjects. Those arriving with little formal schooling or with a history of failure are often evaluated as underachievers. Inevitably, their lack of confidence is reinforced; while the absence of their formal training is objectively uncovered, their non-academic accomplishments and experience may not be discovered, let alone recognized.

Still other difficulties arise when curricula are designed for adult basic education. Even though the entering students have much to learn, educators are obliged to pare down the programs because of the pressure of time and the lack of money. Subject matter that normally takes years of schooling is streamlined, simplified, and compressed. A sort of telescopic teaching style is developed in which large areas of North American basic skills are cut up into segments. Speed is all important. The aim is to have students pass, as quickly as possible, the examinations thus equipping them with the certificates that everyone hopes will improve their position in the job market. Whereas full-time college undergraduates are dissuaded from cramming, community students must per force hurry through their mini-courses. This ingurgitation of prepackaged knowledge precludes any creative, pleasurable experience of learning; no time is allocated to the slow, strenuous, but educational process of comprehending, a process that allows newly acquired knowledge to become really meaningful and related to experience.

These programs have been useful in establishing centers where newcomers can find some initial training and where dropouts could get another chance. However, people often hesitate to avail themselves of the offered opportunity; they are apprehensive of the placement tests, of the competition, of the classroom where their lack of education might be publicly exposed. Many of those who do find the courage to get started lose heart somewhere along the way, begin to miss classes, and fall behind. Others graduate but cannot find a way of relating what they have learned in class to what happens in the outside world. Fear of not succeeding, the scarcity of available work, discouragement at having to begin as an adult from scratch at an elementary level are additional factors that will, time and again, bring a large number of adult students to the brink of despondency and failure.

My own involvement in some of these programs led me to wonder whether adults who join these programs could be reassured about their capacities and strengthened in their resolve. Could one show that past experience can become a resource? Could persons unused to academic learning be given the hope that they could exercise and improve their critical abilities? Could voices often silent be encouraged to speak up and self-assurance increased? Could a new energy be released through an active participation in an activity where new knowledge becomes readily related to life experience? Was there a space that would be favorable to this opening up?

A personal recollection stands out in my own mind. During my work as an instructor in a skill-training agency in Dorchester, Massachusetts, I became acquainted with a Puerto Rican man, recently arrived from the island. He was one of the people to whom we taught the skills needed to measure and lay linoleum on floors. I was in charge of the English needed for this job. One day, during a lunch hour, I was surprised to see him draw tropical landscapes with colored chalks on the blackboard of one of the classrooms. We began to chat about his life in a small Puerto Rican town. He told me with great gusto how he had managed to feed his family in Puerto Rico by becoming a clever entrepreneur. He somehow rented a truck, picked up vegetables from different small growers at dawn, and resold them later in the market. His story was full of amusing asides that made both of us laugh. Sadly, I must report that this same voluble and resourceful person performed badly when a potential employer came to interview him. Partly his talents were not recognized by a standard North American employment questionnaire and partly he did not have the confidence that he needed to express himself effectively in this new environment.

The experience with Juan and his reference to Noah as he came into contact with Arguedas' story as well as my conversations with the man in the skill training center, were dramatic examples that people with little conventional schooling had a knowledge perhaps different from our own but valuable and interesting— people have lived full, sometimes complex lives, they have also heard stories from elders, have read the Bible and can sing lots of songs, quote proverbs, improvise popular poems.

These encounters and other similar ones prompted me to reflect on how one could make learning more meaningful, especially for persons who lack the self-confidence that comes from classic schooling. Was there a way to utilize the experience acquired during daily life? Could new knowledge be incorporated in what was already familiar? Was there a space where common knowledge could interact with the more sophisticated products of our culture?

ORIGINS

A five-year stay in Colombia in the fifties brought me in contact with new cultural groups. I discovered a creativity which was not always built on a discipline acquired in schools. I learned to appreciate ingenuity, playfulness, imagination, and a kind of mental energy that displayed itself in a multitude of ways—not only in museums and books but also in carvings on the walls of churches, in ceramics displayed in market stalls, in songs and dances during fiestas, in the exuberance of street language.

Latin American authors were speaking in new voices and becoming more attentive to their own continent, less immersed in the fashions of the European avant-garde. García Márquez, for example, was just beginning to develop the style which was to become known as "magic realism." The literature which he and other authors were creating seemed to capture the illusive qualities of a world that captivated me. I began to read and study their works.

PAULO FREIRE

A 1969 seminar given at Harvard University by the Brazilian philosopher and educator Paulo Freire introduced me to his thought and to his work on literacy in the Northeast of Brazil. Freire was convinced that people could acquire new knowledge only as it becomes meaningfully related to their life. Literacy sessions organized by him and his students were therefore always preceded by dialogues on subjects that held a special interest to those who were learning to read. Thus, in an arid region of Brazil, a sketch of a simple well, projected on a white wall, generated a discussion that locked persons in a debate not only about water but also about land, its ownership, water control, and so on. Dialogues on such "generative" themes preceded the actual, more technical, literacy sessions that then focused on words related to the previously debated issues. A "conscientization," consciousness-raising, occurs as people deepen the understanding of their condition and attempt to improve their control over it; people gain a new assurance and become actively engaged in a learning process which supplants what Freire contemptuously dismisses as "banking" education where teachers deposit new information which they deem important into the minds of accepting, passive students.

Freire's practical work and persuasive thought helped me appreciate the power of genuine dialogue. I came to understand how persons with limited education could discuss themes that were meaningful to them. I also began to ask myself how this Freirean approach could lead to critical thinking in other areas. And then, one day, during a seminar session, I asked myself: could a beautiful, multivocal, short story exercise similar powers to Freire's projections? Could a literary text stimulate the imagination and set in motion a number of links to some private experiences? And could members of a group who read and discuss a story together transform these deeply felt private reactions into a more public discourse that could become a dialogue? I became quite fascinated by this possibility and decided to test it in the real world. Moreover, the possibility of such an enterprise attracted me because it satisfied my own interests as it would allow me to combine my taste for reading literature with my wish to develop a better way to communicate with a larger group of people than the highly educated.

The Freire seminar convinced me that sophisticated and critical dialogues could occur among a much greater variety of persons once their interest was engaged—the projected picture of a well was sure to start a discussion among people who lived in a land where water was so crucial. But could varied, richly textured literary works, not clearly focused on immediate preoccupations, be a good source of "generative themes"? Would persons without formal education be capable of participating in dialogues about themes and characters encountered in novels, short stories, poems? Would they become real "readers" and be sensitive to the images, metaphors, rhythms of the poetic texture?

While Paulo Freire himself always liked the Gente y Cuentos concept, some of his disciples who often tended to be more doctrinaire than Paulo, have objected to the use of works of fiction as both too remote and too complex for groups whose concerns appear removed from literature; they denounced them as creations of sophisticated, "high culture" authors who express their own domineering views inimical to a "conscientization" process which should lead to a critical reflection on self and one's relation to society.

And yet, the authors who often have gone to the people for their initial inspiration are, in a sense, similar to Freire's researchers of generative themes: both have done field work, both have looked and listened, both have identified the important themes.

Freire's disciples translate these themes into simple, poster-like suggestive drawings which elicit intense reactions from persons who recognize their significance. Writers, on the other hand, transform these themes into fiction and into a narrative which has its own very different way of reaching out.[4] Literary texts not only offer themes that may be familiar and relevant, they also open up entirely new ways of exploring them by stimulating an imaginative boldness.

My speculative questions were also criticized by my academic friends. How could uneducated minds who had not read much understand and discuss sophisticated writers? I was accused of being both utopian and populist.

Moreover, and sadly, it must be recognized that less educated persons themselves often become convinced that the humanities are not "for them." They perceive literature, of which they often have not had any experience, as a somewhat mysterious area of high culture from which they are barred forever because of their particular background.

Thus, both students and educators share a basic attitude of discouragement about the possible prospects of certain important, enjoyable educational experiences, and secretly harbor a conviction that at best only modest and limited technical goals can be achieved.

---

4   *Dead Souls*, the extravagantly fantastic novel of Gogol, was preceded by a painstaking preparation during which the author conducted a survey of the speech and ways of the people of Ukraine.

OTHER THINKERS

Yet, I believe my approach is related to what certain social scientists have described as they observed how improvement, development, and growth can occur in unexpected ways and as they noted and analyzed the curious detours of slow round about searches which had been dismissed by other theories as mistaken deviations from the royal way to a well defined goal.

In economics, Albert Hirschman whose *Strategy of Economic Development* opened up new ways of perceiving how growth occurs, has been especially interested in successful but seemingly "wrong-way-round" sequences. In his book *Getting Ahead Collectively*, he describes a number of grassroots experiences in Latin America and shows how improvements in the quality of life are often reached through unexpected routes: security of tenure did not turn out to be a prerequisite for building better houses, the organization of a cooperative preceded the establishment of a school, an innovative intergenerational agricultural program helped private family relations.[5]

Similarly, Amartya Sen together with his collaborator Jean Drèze, have insisted in various works on the complexity of social factors in economic development. For example, at a conference entitled "Economic Development, Public Action and Social Progress" Jean Drèze described how in the Indian state of Kerala, an impressive decrease in child mortality was achieved through a determined public policy toward female literacy consonant with the ancient local tradition of matrilineal kinship.[6]

---

5   Albert O. Hirschman. *The Strategy of Economic Development.* New Haven: Yale University Press. 1958. *Getting Ahead Collectively.* New York: Pergamon Press. 1984.
6   Jean Drèze and Amartya Sen. *Hunger and Public Action.* Oxford: Clarendon, 1989. Jean Drèze, "Economic Development,

Robert Putnam's *Bowling Alone: Democracy in America at the End of the Twentieth Century* has captured the imagination of his readers by showing the importance of social connectedness, which he feels is now on the decline. He states "No doubt the mechanisms through which civic engagement and social connectedness produce all these miraculous results—better schools, faster growth, lower crime, more effective government, and even longer lives—are multiple and complex."[7]

The recognition that the multiple and the complex need to be carefully observed is at the center of Clifford Geertz's writings. In his book, *After The Fact*, he eloquently reminds us that it is useless to hope that hard facts can be drawn on to help us understand the "swirls, confluxions, and inconstant connections" that surround us and that "floundering through mere happenings and then concocting accounts of how they hang together..." is a better way to understanding.[8]

Closer to my own subject, studies at the University of Indiana and at the University of Massachusetts in Dartmouth found that serious offenders who were put through a twelve-week literature seminar were less likely to commit new crimes than a control group that had not participated in the discussion of such works.[9]

Public Action and Social Progress," *Canadian Journal of Development Studies*. Vol. XV, No. 3, 1994.

7   Robert D. Putnam. "Bowling Alone: Democracy in America at the End of the Twentieth Century," Noble Symposium : "Democracy's Victory and Crisis," Uppsala, Sweden. 1994.

8   Clifford Geertz. *After The Fact*. Cambridge, MA: Harvard University Press. 1995, pp. 2-3.

9   Michael Ryan. "Read A Book--Or Go To Jail." *Parade Magazine*. NY Post, February 5, 1995.

NEW READER RESPONSE

My desire to understand better how literary works might be received by a new audience, one that had never had access to them, prompted me to study the critics who were interested in reception theories. While various scholars speculated about the relationship of reader and text, very little could be found that helped me answer questions about grassroots audiences as studies about so called "naive" readers never examined individuals below the college freshmen level!

Still, I tried to glean what I could from critics who were particularly attentive to the reader-text dynamic. The early work of Louise M. Rosenblatt (1937) analyzes with great sensitivity the process that takes place as a reader encounters a text and which she calls "transaction." She shows how life history, present preoccupations, as well as wishes and dreams influence how different individuals perceive a work and how people may feel differently about the same short story. Rosenblatt who has worked for many years with schoolteachers is also interested in exploring how such individual receptions can be shared and discussed. Her pioneering work has been mostly influential in schools and has been late in receiving the recognition that it deserves by literary critics. Her many insights have helped me to extend her analysis to the dynamic of the interplay between literary texts and grassroots audiences. I began to ask further questions about how exactly these transactions might occur, how a literary text could best be introduced to a group of people who are not familiar with these kinds of writers, how to encourage an interchange between a person's life experience and a literary text. To get a broader understanding of this dynamic, I decided to turn to a number of critics, psychologists, and philosophers with these questions in mind.

The Russian critic Mikhail Bakhtin is particularly interesting. In examples drawn from English, German, and Russian novels, Bakhtin shows how different "voices" and different points of view can coexist within a paragraph, sometimes even within a sentence. What at first sight appears as a seamless text turns out upon examination to be a collage of diverse visions made to interact in the linguistic space they share. Bakhtin's ingenious analysis shows how a "conversation" is orchestrated between various speech-styles coming from different psychological and social worlds. This ability to incorporate disparate, sometimes antagonistic elements and to bring them to interact gives fiction a special power to motivate readers to face up to complex situations often not so different from their own. Bakhtin's concept of "polyphony" suggests that encounters with fiction are indeed likely to produce unusual dialogues inspired by the different thematic threads that intermingle.

Others like Paul Ricoeur (*La métaphore vive*), Roland Barthes (*Le plaisir du texte*), Philip Fisher, Viktor Shklovskij, Boris Eichenbaum, Jurij Lotman, taught me how to look at texts with a more discerning eye. My more specific interest on how inexperienced readers might react brought me to consult a number of critics of the German Konstanz School. Wolfgang Iser's (*The Act of Reading*) work has been particularly useful as well as the writings of Hans Robert Jauss. As I immersed myself in different theories, I profited from the work of Jonathan Culler, Mary Ann Cows, Mary Louise Pratt, Tzvetan Todorov, Robert Scholes, Susan Suleiman, Hans Georg Gadamer, Michel de Certeau (*L'invention du quotidien*) among others. But sitting at my desk and enjoying the interesting elaborations of these scholars was not enough. The experiment of bringing grassroots audiences in touch with literary works had to take place out there, in the barrios, churches, community centers.

A NEW VENTURE

The program began in 1972 as Gente y Cuentos and acquired its title People and Stories/Gente y Cuentos after sessions in English were started in 1986.

A stroll to a low income housing project in Cambridge, MA, led me to an inner courtyard where several young Latina women were sitting on their stoops minding their children. My years in Colombia allowed me to address them easily in Spanish: would they like to help me organize a new activity in the meeting room of their building? It would deal with their own "cultura." Perhaps they had not had a chance to finish school but would still like to know something about their Latin American authors who wrote in Spanish? Did they know that many were now such a big hit and translated into English? The women had never heard of these writers but responded almost immediately to the "own cultura" argument. It did not take long to get a group together and a few days later seven women gathered around a table to hear and discuss "La siesta del martes" ("Tuesday Siesta") by Gabriel García Márquez.[10] Right from the start I could see that the enterprise would be successful! Of course, much remained to be worked out: how to handle the active children who distracted the mothers, how to find more stories, how to improve the questions that would move the dialogue along, but the women were talking, enthusiastic about the tough determination of the mother in the tale, surprised to recognize how similar her concerns were to their own. The participants did not all agree, yet a bond of understanding and warmth emerged as the group identified a world they knew in this unfamiliar Colombian story printed in a book. Moreover, the vibrant language delighted the women who recognized expressions and terms known since childhood,

---

10   Gabriel García Márquez. "La siesta del martes." *Los funerales de la Mamá Grande*. Xalapa, México: Universidad Veracruzana, 1962.

rich with connotations. Smiles of understanding were exchanged and moments of misunderstanding or differences were shared without too much tension. In fact most enjoyed the digging into the arguments, the cooperative intellectual effort. The story helped open up exchanges about experiences and memories. The fact that it was "just a story" provided the necessary distance. Difficult issues could be brought up that were excluded from daily conversations, and painful experiences could be relived safely, linked to a story that had familiar resonances but was not quite their own.

The success of this first informal gathering gave me plenty of courage to pursue my project. How could I convert this heady first experiment into a program that could be developed into a durable enterprise and be shared with others? I continued on my own, experimenting for quite some time before attempting to draft the lines of a more formal program. Was it possible to give some semblance of a structure, to draw up a methodology that would provide an adequate umbrella to the disparate, small dramatic happenings that took place during the different sessions? I decided to try, so I could begin to work with others, and enlarge the scope of this experiment. As a start, to organize my thinking, I decided to define separately the three actors – the story, the participants of the group who were discussing it, and the coordinator who helped to make it all happen.

PHOTOS

Gente y Cuentos, first meeting in Trenton, NJ, 1972

"Graduation", Mompós, Colombia, 2009

People and Stories, Operation Fatherhood, Trenton, NJ, 2009

Gens et Récits, Rural Elders, southwest France, 2007

Gente y Cuentos in Children's Home Society, New Jersey, 2009

Locked in discussion, Crossing Borders, Trenton, NJ, 2009

A fun moment, Crossing Borders, 2009

Deep inside the story, Bogotá, Colombia, 2009

Participants in a barrio near Buenos Aires, Argentina, 1984

THE ACTORS: STORIES, COORDINATORS, GROUPS

STORIES

SELECTION

Right from the start, I had decided that I wanted to introduce new readers to outstanding literary works, to texts that would spark the imagination, affect feelings, arouse intellectual curiosity and stimulate individuals to wonder, to search, to offer their opinions, to relate those writings to their own lives. As in a play, I wanted each session to open the curtain on a work that could be enjoyed in its entirety, where people could experience a complete composition, its beginning, the development of its themes, its inner tensions, its end sometimes surprising, disturbing, sometimes reassuring, and conclusive.

The literary genre of the short story came immediately to mind as eminently suitable, especially at the time that I was beginning to develop the program when many talented Latin American writers were publishing wonderful short stories. The length of ten pages or so of many of them could be read aloud in ten to fifteen minutes and was therefore particularly suitable for sessions of one and a half to two hours, leaving plenty of time for a leisurely discussion. Moreover, community groups are not always completely stable and attendance may vary slightly from one time to another; it is therefore best to present a complete work at each session. In any event, as Cortázar[11] says "Short stories…are living creatures, complete organisms, closed circles, and they breathe" – surely their organic structure should never be truncated.

So a session always begins with the reading aloud of a complete short story. Participants just listen to the reading or if they wish, follow the text on the copy that was distributed to them at the start of the meeting. The story is not distributed beforehand and is heard for the first time when it is read aloud. This is to avoid possible preparation at home by the more sophisticated members of the group whose level of education might inhibit other less educated participants during the face to face discussions. It is also for this reason that the story is read by the coordinator rather than by the participants themselves.

Gradually, bibliographies of stories of suitable length in Spanish, French, and English have been developed—the result of many hours of labor—and new coordinators can readily find what they need in those lists. Opinions vary on the use of translations. At first, I created bibliographies which listed exclusively stories written in their original language. Their images, metaphors, poetic texture seemed to me more apt to evoke memories, touch the imagination and the emotions of the native speakers. But over the years, various coordinators wanted to offer stories from a wider circle of cultural groups, so stories translated from various

---

11   Cortázar, Julio. "Del cuento breve y sus alrededores." *Último round.* México, Siglo XXI Editores, 1969 (my translation).

European, Asian, African, American languages were added to our repertoire and now our bibliographies list a number of great international stories in translation that seem to work well enough.

Another initial consideration to be taken into account when choosing a story is its complexity. We never shorten stories or attempt to simplify them in any way. The text is presented just as the author wrote it. So if after a first reading a story seems just too complex, uses too many learned references or perhaps appears too abstract, we may want to leave it aside. However, gauging whether a story will be accessible is not an easy task. Some wonderful, poetically rich stories will perhaps be too difficult. For example, while "Emma Zunz" by Borges[12] has provoked spirited discussions, other great stories by him would probably seem too abstract. In order not to lose our inexperienced public, something in the story, even during a first reading and before the discussion takes place, must catch the interest of the participants. Language that is too strange, references that are too esoteric may create an initial discouragement that will be hard to overcome. Also certain subjects may be too embarrassing to discuss in a group of persons who do not know each other, although much depends on the skill of the coordinator and we must remember that participants often can handle far more than we presume.

But once a tentative choice of story has been made, how can we be sure that our first, almost intuitive decision to introduce it to a group is going to work? How much should we think about the composition of the group with whom the story is to be discussed?

Very different people take part in those discussions. When a group is formed we usually have only a vague (and sometimes

12   Jorge Luis Borges. "Emma Zunz." *El Aleph.* Buenos Aires, Emecé Editores, 1957.

mistaken) idea of the capacities or desires of the persons who join. Rather than trying to interview participants before the start of the program, and try to guess what they will enjoy, I prefer to allow the story to do its work and engage the imagination and curiosity of the readers. The results are often unexpected and revealing. In any event, it would be presumptuous for us to try to predict what others desire, what others are really interested in. I'll never forget how astonished I was at the reaction of one of the participants in a discussion held in an extremely poor barrio outside of Buenos Aires. We were exchanging remarks after reading a story by the Argentinean writer Daniel Moyano,[13] dealing mostly with a couple of actors falling out of love. At one point, one young woman said "You know what my greatest wish is for our barrio? I would like just once, just once, to have a ballet group come to perform here." Who could have predicted such an unexpected and precise longing in a barrio that lacked even clean water, and proper sewers? So trying to tailor the story to an audience is probably both presumptuous and useless.

One often hears that reading material for older people should be gentle, optimistic, preferably dealing with memories. But is it really so? Actually, we have found that it is the toughness of the old woman who refuses to be defeated by her physical problems in Eudora Welty's "The Worn Path" that interested and pleased a group of Senior citizens. Older participants sometimes begin by resisting stories with too much turmoil—they're not supposed to like that—but in fact they enjoy being drawn into an interesting discussion no matter what the subject and they are pleased to contribute to the conversation, to hear themselves on unexpected subjects. They appreciate being treated as intelligent individuals rather than as fragile old dears who need to be protected from too much excitement.

---

13   Daniel Moyano. "Artistas de variedad." *La espera y otros eventos.* Buenos Aires: CEAL, 1987.

Similarly, people who are incarcerated don't necessarily want to hear about violence and crime. For them stories can open windows to the outside, help them reflect and talk about a variety of subjects. A story like "Searching for Zaabalâwi" by the Egyptian writer Naguib Mahfouz[14] that describes a mysterious quest for some loving character, can provoke a moving exchange about hope, about a future out of prison.

So if things are so unpredictable, can we still establish some useful criteria for choosing stories?

One rapid, fairly dependable experiment to see whether a story is suitable is to look whether it offers a number of "shadows." Even a cursory reading with this question in mind will help put aside stories that are too didactic and therefore unable to stimulate the imagination. Hopefully, an experienced reader will also notice, even during a first perusal, whether the story has poetic qualities: are different voices heard, are there unexpected twists in the narrative, interesting oppositions, striking images? But the initial "shadow" test is perhaps the most convenient one; stories with crystal clear didactic messages will probably not yield an interesting discussion and might as well be discarded from consideration.

CRITICAL WORK

Initially I would go to meet the group confident that a good, exciting story would surely generate a lively dialogue in a group. But I soon realized that I could not always count on such an easy success. To be ready to introduce a story and to coordinate a dialogue, a thorough preparation was necessary. As I tried to

14   Naguib Mahfouz, "A la recherche de Zaabâlawî." *L'amour au pied des pyramides.* Paris, Babel, 2002.

put some order in this process, and to think of others who would be working with me, I decided for clarity's sake, to divide that preparation into three parts. A first private intimate reading of the chosen story, a second more critical rereading, and a third one dedicated to planning and formulating possible questions.

First, we must immerse ourselves in the story, read and reread it for our own pleasure and understanding. Let our imagination fly, give free rein to our own emotions. Savor the interplay of the characters, the images, and the language; try to become as familiar as possible with the story, enjoy it as much as we can.

In a second movement, we must take our time and return to the text in a more critical way, rereading it closely, trying to understand its structure, its specific characteristics, its poetic language.

To help new coordinators who are not necessarily experienced literary critics to get a better grip on the text, I devised some simple categories that might serve as a convenient way to organize this part of the work on the story. Those loose categories simply serve to get started and help sharpen and order the multiple and sometimes tumultuous reactions to the story. I named them Poetic Landscape, Contrasts and Confrontations, Shadows, and Themes. To launch the work, I found some simple techniques quite useful: four separate sheets of paper should be made ready to collect notes made on each category as the text is combed during this critical preparation. Having those notes on separate sheets will make it easier later on to construct appropriate open ended questions that will help participants not only to understand the story better, but also to relate it more meaningfully to their own experience and sensitivity.

To counteract the tendency of less experienced coordinators to concentrate exclusively on the themes, on what the story seems to be about, I suggest to begin with the Poetic Landscape category, searching for Contrasts and Shadows next, and leaving Themes for last. This order imposes a certain discipline which sharpens the sensitivity to the texture of the story and helps to notice its literary qualities while avoiding getting lost in a premature discussion of its issues and themes.

Finally, in a third movement, we turn our mind to how we will present the story to the group: what kind of questions might be asked to launch the discussion? What others will best act as bridges between the story and the different personalities of the group? What questions will best help them to draw on their own life experience in order to get more deeply into the text, to understand it better, to live it in a more profound, a more enjoyable way and to make it more relevant?

The initial critical work done during the preparation of the story in the privacy of our study will suggest a number of possible fruitful, generative questions that are likely to spark and sustain dialogues. However, we must humbly accept that all of our careful planning might have to be modified during the actual session as the reactions of the participants may take us on a very different path; listening attentively to those reactions, responding to them is essential. Nevertheless I have found that a strong preparation helps and contributes to a sense of security which makes it easier to remain attentive to the various things said in the group and to be able to improvise and follow up on unexpected reactions. Most importantly, it also helps to keep the dialogue within bounds and related to the story.

FOUR CATEGORIES

The four categories mentioned above, Poetic Landscape, Contrasts and Confrontations, Shadows, Themes, are used to help coordinators organize their thoughts about the story. They are in no way impervious to each other and may often appear too mechanically separated. Nevertheless they serve as a loose net that can capture important details of the text and assist the coordinator/critic as she plunges into the detailed preparation of a story.

Poetic Landscape

A poetic work does not "tell" its story in an orderly, didactic fashion. Sudden beginnings and inconclusive ends, strangely assembled bits of dialogue and narrative, voices that intermingle, conversations that seem to come from different sources, words that echo each other, slightly different versions of what at first seemed simply repetitions, unexpected images and comparisons, adjectives that bite or soothe, clichés that mimic to subvert, are all part of the process through which a literary story comes to be. This vivid unusual language of fiction surprises and delights. It may also confuse but it always keeps us alert.

These intricate and mobile atoms of fiction buffet the reader, who is trying to structure the impressions she/he receives. Our own life experience offers some supporting poles which allow us to begin to scaffold our impressions. But the story may carry us off elsewhere, bring us to altogether new horizons, or even transport us into imaginary worlds.

The deepening of understanding of a story is attained not only through debates of issues. A couple of words nested in a sentence may upset equilibrium. Why are they there? How do they affect us? Similarly a recurring repetition, a cliché that becomes comical in a certain context, a fresh metaphor, an unusual turn of speech or one that is especially familiar, are all important stopping points that may open unexpected vistas. Fiction, as the Russian critic Bakhtin has so powerfully said, creates vast worlds where many forces intersect, where clusters of dissimilar voices can coexist and confront each other, where we can perhaps begin to penetrate without fear a complexity that resists both daily common sense and analytic thought.

For example, in the Puerto Rican story, "En el fondo del caño hay un negrito" ("There's a Black Child in the Ditch"), by José Luis González,[15] a woman who lives in a shack at the edge of a shanty town built over stagnant water, explains that she had to come there because she was displaced by an urban development that was recently built in San Juan. The story at first sight seems to be a powerful condemnation of misguided planning, a plea for social justice for the poor. Yet the story starts with what appears as a free-floating episode of an infant who, early in the morning, crawls toward a pool of water where he sees his reflection and smiles at it. The same scene occurs again at noon and finally at sundown when the child smiling again, reaches out to his own reflection and drowns. The three episodes are initially perceived as incidental, exterior to the main framework of the story. True, it is the hunger of the boy Melodía that finally drives his unemployed father to attempt to find a few hours of work so he can bring food to the child who has not had milk for days. True, some of the characteristics of shanty town society come to light as the relatively better-off inhabitants of this very poor community manage to help the newly-arrived parents to feed their child. The three poetic vignettes of Melodía looking at his own reflection seem to superimpose themselves as lyric fragments that remain separate from the earthy character of the rest of the tale. Yet we intuit that the remoteness is only apparent and that the story wants us to open up to a coexistence of these different threads in the story. The insistent repetition of the Melodía motif, told three times in a story that is only a few pages long, the combination of the sweetness of the child with his tragic drowning at the

15   José Luis González. "En el fondo del caño hay un negrito," *En este lado*. México: los presentes, 1954. Also in *Todos los cuentos*, México: UNAM, 1992.

end, the counterpoint between the futile efforts of the father and the charm of the unconcerned infant, give the episode great emotional impact.

Melodía appears three times. "Three" evokes visions of magic and of reverence in religion as well as in folk tradition. Listeners need not be particularly learned to respond to the three-time recurrence of the Melodía motif and to sense that something important and almost sacred is taking place when the child appears on the scene.

There are other clues: Melodía is not a saint's name. He appears as a being that is not quite real; he can remain sweet and unconcerned like a song, like his name. Melodía ends his life because he is ignorant. He mistakes his reflection for another child and drowns; and yet the feeling lingers that the accident is not all heartbreaking. María, one of the participants, says, "He'll be lifted up and carried to heaven by the angels!" Melodía drowns as he extends his hand in a gesture of friendship and love toward another little black boy. His innocent life and his sudden death remain sweet, untainted, beyond the reach of the squalor that surrounds him.

Melodía's drowning will surely remind a more sophisticated reader of the Narcissus myth, but the episode can also open itself in other, less learned ways. The search for an answer, the enigma of the other, the quest for love, the danger of wanting to reach out too quickly to the unknown, of wanting to capture a true reflection of self are all "poetic" themes suggested by a number of mirror incidents. The woman (she is nameless) scrutinizes the expression of her husband as he comes to her hungry for sex. Is he drunk again as he was the first time that he possessed her? Can she make him less aggressive? The woman finds no answer in the eyes of the man. This ambiguous exchange of looks between man and wife initiates the dialogue in the group: 'When a man is drunk, his eyes are wild, but they are also veiled." "It seems that the woman here is not really his wife that he is only looking for a wife." Participants begin to talk about themselves indirectly as they are moved by the images in the text. They search for answers in the poetry of the text, in the variations on the theme – looks, glances, misapprehensions. A motorist going to work in the morning sees the slum from the bridge, high above, as on a television screen, a clear image yet so distant and unreal, while the father from his shack sees the motorist as a man who has it all and shouts a profanity at him "carajo," fuck you, don't you understand? That aggressive, vulgar term provokes lots of comments about cars passing by with windows shut and doors well locked, zooming through town, fearing contacts with less well-off groups, about misconceptions of life in the "inner city," and an ever widening conversation about living in vastly different circumstances. The use of strong, even abusive language of the father often brings people to disagree on available ways to resist or protest. Is street language ever acceptable, functional? When is it permitted to say things that we were told by our families we should not say?

Toward the end of the story, a scene illustrates how everyday language can function in a different way, how it can reinforce bonds between persons and help solve difficulties. A worker on the wharf lends his wheelbarrow to Melodía's father as he must run off to assist his own wife who is about to give birth to "one more poor devil to join this world." The two men commiserate and conclude with a bit of chitchat and a consoling saying: "Mañana será otro día" (Well, tomorrow is another day). Here a well-worn, popular expression brings two strangers together, although lending of the wheelbarrow also helps, of course! With it the father can earn a few coins as he helps unload some merchandise from a boat. Participants often like this scene. They enjoy the bittersweet flavor and make jokes about consoling formulas, about the reference to the midwife, about those children that keep coming! People may not know about Narcissus or any other Greek myths, but they can feel close to the poetry of the González story.

It is easy to see from the above examples that Poetic Landscape is only a loose category meant to help the reader pay attention to the texture of fiction. As the coordinators prepare themselves for the session, lists of these poetic highpoints made during the critical working out of the story will prove invaluable in helping to formulate questions meant to steer the group participants to notice and to open up to these passages.

The next two categories, Contrasts and Shadows can really be considered as subdivisions of Poetic Landscape. However, for pedagogical reasons, they can be helpful in perceiving somewhat different points of interest in the poetic texture of the text.

Contrasts and Confrontations

A literary text brings concepts, words, and images to confront each other in unexpected and vigorous ways. Tensions are generated that emphasize contrasts and similarities. This confrontation of forces generates an energy that acts on the imagination, which then begins to splinter and recast what it encounters. As we try to reconcile contrasts or become aware of the dramatic need to accept sometimes irreconcilable oppositions, we are drawn to become active players in the text that incites us to question and respond.

When in "La siesta del martes" ("Tuesday Siesta")[16] Gabriel García Márquez begins with the description of the unbearable heat in an unnamed Colombian village, he tells us something about everyday life on the Caribbean coast but there is also more to his

---

16   Gabriel García Márquez. *Los funerales de la mamá grande.* Universidad Veracruzana, México 1962. In English, *No One Writes to the Colonel and Other Stories,* New York: Harper& Row, 1968.

tale. In that story, a woman accompanied by her daughter, takes a long train trip to a small town where her son, Carlos Centeno, has been killed in murky circumstances and buried without an inquest. The mother is intent on accomplishing the necessary last rites and deposit flowers on the tomb of her son. To do so, she must first obtain the key to the cemetery which the priest in charge is not anxious to give her. The confrontation is dramatic but in the end she manages to accomplish what she came to do. In a different kind of program one might use the story as a catchy introduction to an educational social studies session on the Caribbean region. Notions of geography, sociology, economics would be brought in and some of that information might be useful both from the point of view of introducing basic data to a group that has not learned about it in school, and of encouraging an exchange of views between persons, many of whom come from that area of the world. But in People and Stories/Gente y Cuentos, helped by the coordinator's questions, the participants may be led in a round about way to approach the story through a series of oppositions. They may be made, for instance, to notice the full dramatic impact of the sun's heat on the characters and on everything that is happening in this village.

The heat in "Tuesday Siesta" provides much more than a setting: it actually becomes one of the forces that activate the story. The implacable sun, the harshness of nature, the hostile surroundings are pitted against the determination of a brave woman whose spirit will not be defeated by difficult circumstances. The impassive woman who rides in a dusty, steamy train without complaining, silent and disciplined, is the very same woman who will stand up later to the authority of the powerful man who tries to deny her the right to deposit the flowers that she brought to lay on the grave of her murdered son. The story emerges through a series of confrontations in which we become emotionally involved, partly because each of us has lived through conflicts somewhat similar to these and partly because the clashes in the story are taking hold of us.

The very first paragraph, that pitches the erect and severe figure of the woman, all dressed in black, against the rays of the sun, prepares our imagination to respond to the dramatic events about to take place. And the woman's ability to disregard the stifling heat in the train that brings her to the village also prepares us to understand her posture as she remains standing and erect, confronting the priest who tries to deny her urgent request. The tensions in the story stir the participants to recall some of their own experiences. María tells about her first job interview: the sweat, the need to look tidy and cool. In a session in Argentina, Jorge recounts how the community decided to confront the dishonest landowner who would not deliver the certificates of ownership to those who had paid for their barrio lot. The dwellers remained firm; the owner would not yield; a forceful "occupation" of the land followed.

Further along, the conflict in the story becomes more focused and more violent and finds its expression in the way that language is manipulated. When the mother says that she has come to the cemetery to look for the grave of the "thief," the word thief produces a shock effect—we expected her to say "son." At times, I even tried to help participants experience the full drama of this moment by suggesting they try "just as an experiment" to call someone they love by an offensive name. The jolt, the scandal produced by certain words when confronted with others, might not only surprise but may almost shatter. Actually no one ever volunteers; people find it impossible to go through with the experiment and the silence in the room attests to the explosive nature of certain terms.

But the craft of the author highlights the unspeakable word and forces us to face up to the drama, to engage our own memories of violence. A build-up occurs that produces a kind of revelation: "thief" pronounced at this point by the mother is an accusation. In our mind it gets immediately contrasted with the word that it would have been normal to pronounce; "thief" instantly triggers "son", the word which we would expect the mother to use; as a result all kinds of associations readily come to mind and "thief" in this context begins to mean its opposite: a man who was somehow defeated by circumstances, a man who was killed as a thief without any proof of his stealing, a man whose grave is unmarked and who has been buried as a criminal without any judicial inquiry, a man who had always been a tender and good son and who is now alone and degraded in death. The word "thief," placed as it is at the apex of the story, coming at that particular juncture, acquires an irruptive power as it appears in counterpoint with the word "son" that we expect. The contrast precipitates a number of powerful images and connotations and it reaches beyond the story, into the lives of people.

Not only does fiction spark memory through dramatic moments, it also has an ability to move it out of its frozen molds. People tend to imprison past episodes of their lives within set frames that become fixed, stored away, or sometimes recounted and "remembered" in conveniently comfortable versions. A poetic text can suddenly jolt these somewhat old images and bring them back to life through unexpected contrasts that shatter the sclerotic memories. "Thief," as pronounced by the Colombian mother may bring up doubts about past relationships with children or lovers. These modifications that are almost forced on us by the text can be confusing, painful, frightening. Certainly sharing them with a group may be sometimes difficult. But the story provides help. While it summons repressed, unclear, conflicting shreds of past experiences, it also offers a way to deal with them. A literary story, told by an author, is not our life; it provides a distance that allows the discussion of sensitive issues and offers a manageable structure that organizes and makes available those new "threatening" insights.

Shadows

A literary story has a life of its own with areas of residual shadows that no amount of clever analysis will eliminate. Ambiguities and a certain mystery will continue to veil some of the edges of the characters and of the plot. These unresolved aspects recall the inconclusive experiences of daily life. This slippery and evanescent quality of fiction disturbs but at the same time tantalizes our imagination[17].

In the last scene of "Tuesday Siesta," the mother disregards all advice to be patient, to wait for sundown. Instead she leaves the parsonage, keys in hand, to proceed to the cemetery, where she intends to accomplish her mission and place the flowers she brought from home on her son's grave. As she comes out of the dark parsonage into the blazing sun, everyone is at their windows watching her, the mother of the "thief." The streets, usually deserted at siesta time, are buzzing with an ominous crowd. What does this end of the story suggest? What does it mean? Are the people of the town simply curious? Are they having second thoughts about the way the town authorities have acted? Do they feel guilty themselves? Are they going to heckle the woman, are they going to support her, or are they simply going to watch her accomplish her mission? The answers to these questions can never be completely settled and often the participants turn over the last page in hope of a clearer answer. In fact, it is the ambiguity that provokes powerful reactions from the group. Mercedes, a Puerto Rican participant, related this last

---

17   New suggestive experiments in psychology show how a reading of an ambiguous story by Kafka can beget an improvement in creative thinking. Proulx, Travis and Steven J. Heine. 2009. *Psychological Science 20*: 1125-1131

scene to Christ's response upon having to judge an adulteress: "If there is one of you who has not sinned, let him be the first to throw a stone at her." Others saw the end as illustrating an instinctive, animal-like fearlessness of a mother who is ready to come to the defense of her son, no matter how awesome the enemy might be. In Argentina, where the tragic disappearance of many young people during the violent years of the military regime is forever engraved in memory, the quest of the mother in "Tuesday Siesta" was seen as particularly poignant. Many spoke of the determination of the Mothers of the Plaza de Mayo, the Argentinean group who for years has marched to demand justice for the disappeared. Those barrio participants knew in their flesh what violence was. They saw the crowd watching the mother as immensely threatening but understood her action in their own way—finding the tomb of your own dead, finding the corpse that belongs to you means to regain control, means to overcome violence, to restore justice.

Themes

Fiction proposes themes through existential situations. Events are described as lived in the world or perhaps seen in dreams. Instead of being didactically set forth, issues become actors in complicated roles. Their enactment in different voices involves us as we follow and participate in the intricacies of various ethical positions. This dramatic presentation gives issues a stirring presence. Different opinions acquire their own logic; discussion and deliberation follow almost naturally. But this dialogue should not become just a bull session; rather it should help structure emotions and discipline reflection on the story. Issues in stories become meaningful to us as we become involved with their development within the framework of fiction. In a group, we not only live the story's main themes, but also tinker with their significance. A multi-vocal literary text does not hand down unequivocal messages. The uncertainty provokes discussion and critical analysis: members of the group challenge each other, demand explanations, try out a number of possible interpretations.

In the Puerto Rican story, "En el fondo del caño hay un negrito" ("There's a Black Child in the Ditch"), by José Luis González,[18] a woman who lives in a shack at the edge of a shanty town built over stagnant water, explains that she had to come there because of an urban development that was recently built in San Juan. The discussants exhibit a range of conflicting reactions: the word "urbanización" (urbanization) is a good word, with positive social connotations, and it has a way of triggering Puerto Rican pride. The notion of shanty town, of "arrabal," with all its disagreeable and perhaps shameful sides, is somehow rejected and "urbanización" wins the first round. Participants comment on how new housing is now built in Puerto Rico to replace ramshackle slums, on how the government takes care of its people. They think of Puerto Rico, of back home, of their country, and life is good and they are proud of their island. But on second thought and as the dialogue develops, where is the woman now who speaks up in the story about urban development? In an unhealthy slum! Gradually some of the members begin to recollect experiences that family members or acquaintances have had with housing authorities. "Urban development," after all, does not always spell improvement and modernization for everyone. People did in fact have to leave their homes and were never able to replace them because of the higher rent in the newly built projects. Nevertheless some still cling to the first optimistic notion: the very word "urbanización" somehow becomes a symbol of their pride and they feel that it must be defended against all odds; they continue to deny the difficulties that may arise in the wake of modernization

18   José Luis González. "En el fondo del caño hay un negrito." *Cuentos puertorriqueños de hoy.* Río Piedras, Puerto Rico: Editorial Cultural, 1985.

because they feel that sustaining the honor of their country is more important at this moment than discussing the problems of economic development. Some even begin to accuse the writer of subversive intentions!

In any event, while personal opinions may continue to differ, perceptions of issues become refined during the discussion. Slogans are replaced by questions; proposals are tempered by the need to explain how they are to be carried out. Newly acquired emotional and intellectual courage helps to distinguish the various sides of a problem and to seek solutions. Improved, more modern housing is of course needed, and everyone knows this; but José Luis González' story steers people to sidestep platitudes, to refine ideas and to ask more precise questions. To whom should one entrust the planning of that new housing? Should old buildings be razed and replaced by new structures, or can some older buildings be rehabilitated? Is it best to use the new, often cheaper prefabricated methods or can local labor participate in the building of the new units? How can improved housing in particular, and economic development in general, be fairly shared among the various social groups?

The issues are brought forth by the fictitious characters in the story but the participants discuss them through the lenses of their own lives. Inexperienced readers find this normal: fiction and life appear as a continuum to many of them. This may be confusing to the more literary coordinator who is faced with persons who do not clearly understand the nature of fiction. But this trust in the narrative can be turned into an advantage. The concept of "truth" and its philosophical complexities need not be insisted upon. Coordinators may simply steer the attention of the readers to the salient poetic details so the story can do its work. "Urbanización" used by the author, is a word carefully chosen by him as heavy with value connotations (the word is comically mispronounced in the text, underlining the uncomfortable distance of the uneducated from the very concepts that are most valued by them); "urbanización" has something to do with modernization, with cleaning up, with building up a more powerful nation. Yet when juxtaposed with the stark, all too real images from the slum world, the meaning of "urbanization" shifts and begins to remind people of glib formulas and empty political promises. These contrasts and confrontations brought to life by the literary text provoke arguments, and also a desire to seek new solutions, new ideas.

Who wins? Perhaps no one and perhaps no one can win. Politicians and city planners are forever debating how problems of public housing are to be tackled. José Luis González' story not only brings up some of those thorny issues but it also dramatically uncovers some of the complexities buried in them. The poetic details, the language of literature, help people shed ready-made notions and lead to fresh discussions of issues that matter to them in their own terms. This is why stories that may appear to focus clearly on certain themes are never discussed in the same way by different groups. Nor will the dialogue necessarily converge only on social concerns. Love, friendship, mystical communication with the dead, the source of artists' inspiration, food, dancing, all these topics will be taken up just as energetically as questions of racial enmities, problems of unemployment, gender roles, or survival in unfamiliar cities. No one teaches the participants of the group what they are supposed to conclude on these questions, for what instructor would have the competence to teach people how they ought to react on these matters? The discussions lead to a better understanding of the complexities, perhaps to an understanding that there are no easy answers, sometimes no answers.

At times, the participants themselves introduce other dimensions to the discussion as they sense that there is more to life than social concerns, that play and spinning of imaginative tales are part of life, as much as the pursuit of "truth." I remember vividly, for example, how a discussion of "Petrolio," a short story by Héctor Tizón,[19] brought Antonio, an Argentinean barrio dweller, to embark on a fascinating, comical account of the family of his Gypsy fiancée; his neighbor María who knew him well, protested: "But Antonio what are you saying, this is not true!" But others in the group shushed her down, "Don't interrupt, let him finish, this is really fun!" And Antonio went on to the delight of everybody, creating an imaginary world that became a playful theater for all those present.

QUESTIONS

After establishing the intimate connection with the text of the short story, and looking at it through the different lenses of our four categories, it is time to think how it might best be presented to our audience, to the participants of the group that we are planning to meet.

Copies of the chosen story are distributed to each participant at the beginning of the session but it is the reading aloud that creates the real excitement and expectation as the curtain opens on the action. Reading the story aloud brings it into the room makes it tangible. The text becomes a participant in the circle.

But how can persons unused to literary works be helped to approach, understand, and enjoy them? How can they be encouraged to come up with their own comments? Ways have to be found to give them the instruments with which they can embark on their own exploration of the story.

Well thought out open-ended questions, coupled with scrupulous listening to what is said by the participants, can orchestrate the process. The person reading the story, the coordinator, must

19   Hector Tizón. "Petróleo." *El jactansioso y la bella.* Buenos Aires: Centro Editor de América Latina S.A., 1972.

establish the right ambience where questions are always opening doors, and are never threatening. The questions play a crucial role as they initiate the conversation, arouse curiosity, and later help to develop the give and take where one person's view of the story becomes modified and enriched by the perceptions of others. Well placed questions help the discussion to oscillate between the participants, the coordinator, and the story itself. The public dialogue that is encouraged weaves a network of connections that gives rise to new thoughts and emotions.

How is such a dynamic initiated and sustained? Questions which call attention to the beacons in the text, not only to its themes and its dramatic characters but also to its poetic texture, repetitions, contiguities, strange links between disparate ideas and images, odd verb tenses, voices from different sources sustain a momentum and give permission to wonder, to question, to imagine. They help participants appropriate the text, allow it to impact their imagination; as different opinions are expressed, discussed, participants think critically, discover the audacity to speculate, to imagine, to dream, to enjoy the poetry of the tale.

It should be said here that silences too are important and some are even essential. One such moment usually occurs when the reading aloud ends. It is good, at that moment, to let the story do its work and not rush too quickly into a discussion. But after a while a well chosen first question should break that silence.

It is useless to launch the conversation with a vague general query such as "Well, how did you like this story?" or "So, what do you think of this end of Tuesday Siesta?" Such overly broad questions, especially when introduced early in the dialogue, can only encourage trite, ready-made responses by the members of the group who talk most easily. Others will sit back and shake their heads in approval or disapproval. Even if a dialogue develops it will certainly deal with some of the most obvious themes of the story. No creative flight of the imagination is likely to occur and probably no real disagreement will be debated.

So how should one start? The first couple of questions are meant to overcome the initial shyness of those participants who fear that their lack of schooling may prevent them from participating in the discussion. They should be both concrete and very simple. Even though they may appear to us as redundant, a few elementary questions are in order just to allow voices to come forward. A first question about the climate in "Tuesday Siesta" makes it possible for even the most timid to say something. I often start with an affirmative statement followed by a few straightforward, precise inquiries. For instance:

> *It seems that the story starts with a trip in a train.*
> *What do the passengers see through the window? Do they see*
> *fields, forests, plantations?*

These very first questions are of a different kind from the ones that will follow, and they can be extremely simple.

But soon after this beginning, we want to bring the participants to become much more adventurous. The work done as we prepared the story will help to generate more searching questions. For example, in the preparation sheet entitled "Themes," we may have noted that only the administrators and the priest have electric fans in their houses. A good question related to this theme might elicit discussion on the poor and the rich, on the different classes, the different groups living in the village. For example:

> *The story talks a lot about the heat, the burning sun and*
> *mentions that only certain people have fans. Who has those*
> *fans?*

And then, to involve participants more intimately into the discussion, to show them that their life experience can help them understand the story better, one might ask:

> *Did any of you ever live in a tropical climate? Or in a small Latin American town?*

People will start talking and they will recall their own experiences. An exchange of memories and opinions will begin to create a new dynamic in the group, and a surprising discovery of the other.

As we continue to mine our preparation sheets for more possible questions, our "Shadow" sheet can suggest questions on the murky scene in Señora Rebecca's house where Carlo Centeno gets killed.

> *According to you what exactly happened in Señora Rebecca's house?*

And this question could again be followed by one involving the experiences of the participants, for example:

> *Have any of you ever been close to a situation where there was a suspicion that a crime had been committed, that something fishy had occurred?*

The sheet on "Contrasts and Confrontations" where we noted the contrasting way of speaking of the mother and the priest suggests:

> *Why do you think that the priest uses such conventional formulas as he faces a mother who has lost her son?*

And this could be followed again by a personal question on the daily use of language:

And have you ever used strong language, what some people call bad language, to make a point to obtain what you wanted?

Such a more personal question, easily relating to daily life often overcomes inhibitions; people begin to give examples of somewhat scandalous, frowned upon words, share juicy expressions of their common language and laugh at them.

Perhaps most important will be questions based on the work done on the Poetic Landscape sheet as they help new readers to savor the literary flavor of the story. Strange word combinations, striking images can be highlighted by rereading passages of the text before asking a question. For example:

The mother says as she talks of the times when her son was a boxer "Every mouthful I ate those days tasted of the beatings my son got on Saturday nights." How can food taste of beatings?

And that again could be followed by a question asking the participants to look at the story through their own lives:

Have you ever had trouble eating after a tragedy? Did your food taste differently?

Another question suggested by our work on the poetic landscape of the story could highlight the extraordinary way that the mother identifies her son as she comes to ask for the key of the cemetery. Again it is good to reread the passage to bring the dramatic words into the room:

"Which grave are you going to visit?" he (the priest) asked. "Carlo Centeno's," said the woman. "Who?" "Carlos Centeno"

the woman repeated. The priest still did not understand. "He's the thief who was killed here last week," said the woman in the same tone of voice. "I am his mother."

After reading the passage, one could ask:

How can a mother refer to her beloved dead son as a thief?

To focus the attention of the group on this word, thief, is most important as it seems to stand almost at the apex of the story – scandalous, shaming the priest, the society, for not having had an inquest. To have participants say the word, taste it, feel it, can help them experience the sensations powerful writing can elicit.

As I plan to meet a group, I find it useful to prepare a list of twenty or so possible questions by mining the four sheets of preparation. I try to think of interspersing questions which tend to refer more directly to life experience so that the participants are encouraged to draw on their own knowledge to better savor and understand the story.

The coordinator's attitude during the discussion is of course most important. Constant attention must be paid to the reactions and concerns of the members of the group; this validates their voices and encourages them to take an active part in the conversation. As a result the questions that were so carefully prepared in advance may not be exactly the ones that will be asked during the session itself. Scenarios developed by the participants as they interact with the story will of course modify any preplanned strategy. Nevertheless, a careful preparation before meeting the group, based on the four categories listed in the preparation sheets, will always provide a solid inventory of questions and will ensure that the various poetic sparks of the text can touch the imagination of the participants.

COORDINATORS

My goal has been to create an approach that can be transmitted so that programs could be organized in a variety of places and coordinated by different persons. A crucial step is of course the choice and training of the persons who will actually run the groups, read the stories, and help propel the discussion.

So who should read the story and who can best spark the discussion? Who can plan the questions, and later encourage and moderate the discussions? The concept of "coordinator" has developed over the years; it is a poor term for the key role that this particular actor performs but we use it for lack of a better one. Teacher or leader connotes school and control; facilitator conveys something mechanical where one person simply releases an preexisting dynamic.

What are the qualities required of a good coordinator? A sensitivity to literary works, an ability to present them through open-ended questions to an unprepared group, a willingness to work in difficult surroundings, a talent to deal with unpredictable circumstances and above all a readiness to listen with respect and to react with intelligence to things said by the group participants. Also a fine balance must be maintained between moderating the discussion of others and becoming oneself a participant in it, not fearing to open up once in a while to others in an honest way. Surely, if we want to avoid assuming the all-knowing teacher role, intervening at times in the dialogue with one's own opinion, is better than the superior silence of those who "know best." To come well prepared is essential, but to be flexible and build on what is actually said in the circle of those present, to encourage a passionate and honest give and take, is the final aim. Participants must feel that they are heard, that their voice matters and that they are authorized to speak. Persons from various backgrounds will respond to somewhat different strands of the story. The coordinator must pick up on what this or that participant contributes so that each voice is heard and validated. And private comments must be brought to interconnect by further questions and channeled into an increasingly complex, public, open and democratic discussion.

At first, my hope was to see community persons fill this role. But as I started to work with others and to think through in greater detail the demanding preparation needed to conduct the sessions, I realized that a person unused to intellectual discipline might become discouraged. I was, at first, deeply disappointed by that realization: was I creating a program where only more educated people would teach others what they ought to think and feel? Was I going to fail the Freirean ideas which had inspired me at first? I happened to be in Brazil as I was mulling over these questions, often reading in the São Paulo newspapers the militant articles of Marilene Chaui, a socially committed philosopher interested in popular education. I decided to seek her advice; half expecting that she would advocate the training of community coordinators as the only socially acceptable course. But she understood the difficulties involved and did not advocate a populist solution. She strongly felt that one of the most valuable and original contribution of People and Stories/Gente y Cuentos was to bring together "high literature" with ordinary, not particularly prepared, readers. Therefore, she suggested that it surely made sense to have on the one hand, a more educated coordinator who introduces the story through a reading and questions and, on the other, participants often richly prepared by their various backgrounds but lacking academic training. This way of organizing the program is consonant with the desire of People and Stories/Gente y Cuentos to provide a hinge that binds together literature and life so a new, quite original dialogue can take place.

In 1986 I decided to organize a workshop and train a number of persons who could collaborate with me. Also after years of working in Spanish, I was ready to branch into English, This new step, the need to develop new bibliographies and to have parallel programs in two languages, brought another dimension to the whole enterprise. The New Jersey Council for the Humanities became interested in my work and began to support the program with yearly grants which allowed us to experiment with even more group configurations, both in Spanish and in English.

Over the years, I have developed an orientation program for new coordinators in the form of a workshop that takes place during a series of meetings with the director of the program acting as an instructor. It takes roughly twenty five hours.

After an overview of the project, a session is simulated with the instructor taking the role of the coordinator and the apprentices simulating a group of participants. Preparation of a story through the lens of the four categories, Poetic Landscape, Contrasts and Confrontations, Shadows, and Themes is practiced as well as the formulation of possible questions. During the workshop, apprentices are asked to prepare a story and lead a group. As much as possible they are made aware of the dynamic developing among the participants. The new coordinators are also given suggestions on how to keep notes and write reports on sessions. Other subjects like criteria for the choice of stories, recruitment of groups, are covered as time permits. It is also important to leave plenty of time to discuss difficulties that can arise either during the discussions of the story or more generally in the dynamic of the group.

GROUPS

It is difficult to describe a typical group taking part in People and Stories/Gente y Cuentos discussions. At first, the program started informally with groups of adults recruited in churches, public housing, restaurants. Anyone who wanted to try it was welcome. Later, we began working with a number of more structured groups and we offered programs in learning and rehabilitation centers, senior citizens groups, prisons, soup kitchens, programs for youths in transition, public libraries; we also started to experiment with inter town, interclass or intergenerational groups, and were able to connect our efforts with universities interested in working in communities. Foundations that are supporting us often want to fund programs in certain locations (for example Newark, Philadelphia, Trenton) or are interested in specific groups (women from welfare to work, transition youth). The recent National Endowment for the Humanities (NEH) grant was specifically earmarked for outreach programs of public libraries in different states of the country.

But wherever they take place, groups have a similar profile. A group of seven to twenty persons gathers in some suitable location, a room in a public library, in a community or senior center, or any other organization that is willing to welcome the program. Participants are invited in and encouraged to sit informally in a circle around the coordinator who soon distributes copies of the story to be discussed and begins to read the story aloud.

Each one of us reacts differently to the hearing of the story. Our own feelings and thoughts bring us to initial private responses during this first reading: perhaps blurred images, a sense that something is taking shape in us now, as revived fragments of memories transform themselves to form new visions. Those first, tentative stirrings of our imagination bring a sense of excitement as we feel an ability to respond, a kind of potential creativity. This rush of somewhat conflicting and still hazy reactions can also disturb—especially those who have no familiarity with the strange power of poetic texts. Have I got it right? Is what is being read too complicated for me? What about all these weird events? Did they really happen?

As the reading ends, there is often a moment of salutary silence as an intimate, private first impression of the story begins to take place. But we are not alone, a group surrounds us, and very soon the realization that others have heard the same story, that others must have thoughts and feelings about the reading begins to impact our first private reactions. Some participants may be somewhat fearful of these others, may not be ready to share their own first intimate reactions and to jump into a public discussion. A skillful coordinator will know how to tread cautiously, how to engage the participants into a conversation which will help them find their voice and draw them into a dialogue without violating their privacy.

If successful the resulting discussion should allow people to begin to share ideas and feelings about the text and themselves. A literary text is both complex and open, it does not propound certain truths, and it does not preach any rigid morality; as people talk about it with others they are brought to entertain hypotheses, to try to explain them to others; critical abilities become sharper. However, this public dialogue is of a very special kind. A literary text does not lend itself to ideological discussions where positions often become increasingly rigid. Rather than forcing us into set positions, a poetic story will usually encourage daring flights of the imagination which in this special climate can even be shared with others. The conversation will somehow always relate both to our own experience and to the story and yet also take off into all kinds of liberating, playful, and joyful unexpected directions. Participants enjoy this new experience of hearing themselves as they create this new kind of dialogue where the literary text becomes the occasion which sparks and sustains an interweaving of private impressions with public debate.

During the first years, participants were mostly persons of similar background. "La prueba" ("The Proof") by the Guatemalan writer Rodrigo Rey Rosa[20] was discussed by a Latino group in Spanish. Alice Walker's[21] "Everyday Use" was a story read with an African American group speaking English. Even though the participants entered the discussion with the feeling that they were going to talk to their own, it soon became clear that, in fact, lots of differences existed within each group. After reading "The Proof" in which a young servant tries to cover up for her employer, a group of Latino women in Newark were not all of one mind about the ethics of her decision. Still, they understood one another easily, especially when comparisons began to be drawn between how it felt to work as a domestic servant in a Latin American country and to have a job in New Jersey.

"Everyday Use," the Walker story, contrasts two sisters: one remains on the farm with her mother, the other leaves for the city. How much must one sacrifice to get an education? Is it worth leaving one's family, uprooting oneself to become better schooled? The African American group in Trenton was divided. But the suspense of the plot, the forceful characters, the outrageously comical language, moved the discussion along in a lively way. Even though people did not always agree, they knew in their bones what the crucial issues were and they felt close to each other.

---

20   Rodrigo Rey Rosa. "La prueba." (Unpublished in Spanish). In English in *And We Sold The Rain*, ed. Rosario Santos. New York: Four Walls Eight Windows, 1988.
21   Alice Walker. "Everyday Use." *In Love and Trouble*. New York: Harcourt, Brace, Jovanovich, 1973.

As different opinions surface and become better articulated, members of the community become increasingly curious about one another. This desire to know more about others seems to intensify when participants surprise each other with unexpected statements. When Juan, the church sweeper, spoke of the rainbow as a mystical sign sent to Noah during the discussion of the Arguedas story, the parishioners of the Mount Carmel church suddenly saw him in a new light. On another occasion, a woman, upon leaving our session, shared with me her astonishment about the remark of a man whom she had known only casually before meeting him again in the People and Stories/Gente y Cuentos circle: "I can't believe what Jorge (he was a guard in a Trenton prison) said about the cage!" She was referring to "Baltazar's Marvelous Afternoon," a story by García Márquez[22] in which a wondrous birdcage plays a key role.

When participants reminisce about past sessions, it is often those "amazing" things said by others that are remembered most vividly: the surprise of discovering that people are not what they seem, the unpredictable bits of dialogues. With this uncovering of differences, a new respect for the opinions of others brings about a questioning of clichés, an opening to new ways of seeing things, a new tolerance.

At one point, I decided to see whether this new attitude of tolerance could make it possible to bring together participants from very different backgrounds or of different generations, persons who do not communicate easily with each other in everyday life. The program also took on a new dimension when, at the suggestion of the director of a Senior Center who wanted to try an intergenerational program in her agency, I started to organize discussions with English-speaking groups. The program

22   Gabriel García Márquez. "La prodigiosa tarde de Baltazar." *Los funerales de la Mamá Grande*. Xalapa, Méjico, Universidad Veracruzana, 1962.

which had been so strongly inspired by Latin America was now becoming more international and its name changed from Gente y Cuentos to People and Stories/Gente y Cuentos. More recently as it started to take on a life in France, it is also known as Gens et Récits.

GROUP CONFIGURATIONS

My first experiments with different group configurations helped me appreciate the complexities of group dynamics. The following are three early examples of structures. As the program developed, great varieties of clusters were organized as listed in the appendix «Profile of groups».

Overcoming barriers across generations

Could adolescents from a local high school have anything to say to the elderly of a Senior Citizen Center in Princeton,[23] New Jersey? Actually a program did already exist in the high school to bring these two groups together which consisted of a monthly gathering where tea was served and where the two generations engaged in polite small talk, friendly but hardly conducive to closer ties. There was also a committee which coordinated a useful

---

23   Princeton is mainly known as the seat of the Ivy League Princeton University. Its stately, beautiful homes often have historic connotations: Washington fought in the area and Einstein lived and worked there. Other sides of Princeton are less well known: old African American and Italian communities have now become neighbors of a new Hispanic enclave. Recent industrial developments along a highway have added a population of apartment dwellers—business people and white collar workers—to the older academic population. As a result of all these changes, the town has become far less homogeneous and both the high school and the Senior Resource Center must deal with new economic and cultural problems in the lives of its members.

service whereby students helped the elderly for modest wages: they shoveled snow, paid bills, straightened out the apartment. Upon describing these duties, young people would often say in a slightly condescending tone: "She is so nice! As I finished, we had some ice cream together!" But did they really get to know this "sweet old lady?" Did the older person say anything beyond the perfunctory and somewhat sentimental "thank you" for the physical help received? I decided to see if the two generations could be brought together in a more meaningful way.

The director of the Princeton Senior Resource Center liked the idea of a People and Stories/Gente y Cuentos intergenerational group and offered to talk to her clients. At the high school, the person in charge of the intergenerational committee promised to recruit some students. Both groups expressed an interest although we also encountered a number of complications. High school students found it difficult to find the time to come to meetings lasting an hour and a half. The school could not incorporate this activity into the curriculum, so students had to find time after school hours. But some worked, others trained in sports. Older people had the time but voiced hesitation: "What do we have in common with these kids? They live in another world! They look at TV all the time. They'll be rough..." Still, most of those approached were willing to try. A time was set; in the afternoon, right after school, the students biked over to the Senior Center. Several people wanted to come only once, "to try"; but we asked both groups to make a commitment—once a week for six weeks. Finally the day arrived. We sat around a table where a few cookies and some cold drinks were set out for the starving young. People clustered together by age but we suggested they mix.

The coordinator read "Tuesday Siesta" in an English translation. Old and young found the story a bit difficult, somewhat exotic. No one in the group had been to Latin America but it did not take long for the story to take hold. The dramatic "thief" uttered by the mother to designate her son brought out all kinds of emotions. Old and young were quick to feel the power of the word in the mother's mouth, but they disagreed quite vehemently on the ethics that she expressed: "I told him never to steal anything that anyone needed to eat, and he minded me." The students were shocked that the mother would qualify her admonition. "One must never steal" said several of them. But some of the older participants, who had lived through the Depression, were much more shaded in their opinion. They told stories about the real poverty that their families had experienced; they felt that it was important to examine each case in its context before pronouncing final moral judgments. How surprising that the old, conventional folks were now defending a more complex, a more daring morality while the young, these loose, "happy-go-lucky" youngsters were so rigidly conventional! People left somewhat puzzled, not knowing quite what they should think of each other. In the next few days, there was a lot of talk about "those kids" on the benches of the little park behind the Senior Citizen Center.

In a second session the discussion of Updike's[24] "Dear Alexandros" helped the group to open up to each other. The story begins with an exchange of letters between a Greek boy and an American middle-class man living in a wealthy suburb. The plot seems at first sight rather straightforward. The man has become a kind of godfather to the poor little Third World child and through the intermediary of an agency, he sends him monthly checks. The boy gratefully acknowledges them and at the same time enlivens his thank you notes with details of his everyday activities. Gradually, life in an extended family in Greece becomes contrasted with the loneliness of the divorced, well-to-do man in Connecticut. The group discussed the difficulties about thanking others for charity or for help, about the influence of the vivid, life-loving accounts

---

24   John Updike."Dear Alexandros." *Pigeon Feathers*. New York, Alfred A. Knopf, 1962.

of the boy on the man so removed from real friendships. Some wondered whether a poor boy in Greece could understand the man's feeling of self-deprecation as he wrote that "the money we give you ...is not a fourth of the money we used to spend for alcoholic drinks." Others in the group spoke of gifts from distant grandparents. A student said that she had joined People and Stories because she never knew her grandparents and wanted to find out what older persons were like.

I later found out that an older woman in this group had asked one of the boys whether he would come and read to her once in a while. A remarkable relationship developed and the student continued to visit her, once a week, till the end of the school year.

The positive experience with the first intergenerational People and Stories/Gente y Cuentos group in English encouraged me to try a similar approach in a different cultural setting.

A Latina counselor in the Trenton[25] High School recruited some students and a social worker in Architects' Housing, a Trenton Senior Center, volunteered to interest some senior citizens. However, the older Latinos expressed a certain amount of uneasiness and did not promise to come. I made several visits

25   Trenton, the capital of the State of New Jersey, is home to many groups and there are various faces to this town. All government services are located there and a stately middle-class residential section extends to the west of the city. Small industries offer employment to people of varied cultural backgrounds. Trenton is also typical of a city that is losing its center; it has many boarded buildings, a lot of trash, dangerous streets. Nevertheless tight, lively communities prosper in enclaves that maintain the spirit of a town that continues to develop: Latino groceries and clubs, African American schools and social centers, churches of many denominations. A community college has built an annex to its central suburban campus near the stately old public library.

to the Center to explain the program individually to prospective members and a group was finally gathered. We decided to hold the meetings in the Senior Center and arranged for the transportation of the students.

This group revealed some special cultural difficulties. Right from the start, I could see that the discussion was developing an unexpected dynamic. The Latino notion of "respeto," respect due to the old, was getting in the way of an open dialogue. Young people remained mostly silent, often with their eyes lowered, averted, while the older folks admonished them on this and that, often pointing a finger at them, mostly telling them how they ought to behave: study more, watch less television, pray more, take care of the old, etc. I would barely finish reading the story, when some of the older more vocal members of the group would start their litany of exhortations, invariably singling out a theme in the text that would fit their purpose. After two unsuccessful sessions, I was ready to give up, but then, on the third week, "Es que somos muy pobres" ("We're really very poor") by the Mexican writer Juan Rulfo,[26] turned things around. Rulfo describes how a flood wipes out an already very poor village. The little boy who tells the story recounts the devastation: houses collapse, trees are uprooted, the harvest is ruined, and cows are carried away with their hoofs sticking out of the turbulent waters. His sharp, not so childish eye catches many details, some of them comical, some of them spiked with earthy sex. He talks about his sisters, about their trysts near the river with too many men, about their outraged father who tries to straighten them out by thrashing them. But in the end the sisters leave. The rumor has it that they have become "pirujas," a Mexicanism for prostitutes. Now, says the boy, the younger sister, the one with the pointed little breasts, is in danger too because her dowry, her calf, has been carried away by the flood. Will she also leave to start a bad life in town?

---

26   Juan Rulfo. "Es que somos muy pobres." *El llano en llamas.* Méjico: Fondo de Cultura Económica, 1955.

Something, probably the juicy word "piruja," helped the young to lift their heads and start talking back to the old folks. Everyone wanted to mouth that word, piruja,—it was funny, not at all Puerto Rican, but clear enough. Did the sisters leave town because of poverty? That was what I had thought when I prepared the story for discussion. But no, said the women in the group, they too were poor and they were no "pirujas"! As everyone began to laugh, tongues loosened and young and old began to search for answers together. The students proposed a psychological explanation for the daughters' flight: it was all really the fault of the father who was unable to express his love, to find a way to talk to his daughters. All he knew was to punish, to invoke morals. Now the young people were really onto something. They began telling the older participants that they were tired of moralizing, that older folks, who sometimes did not even speak English, did not understand the peer pressure that was so difficult to withstand, that they judged them by a set of morals that did not apply in the Trenton high school. All of this was of course answered by the older generation, but all of a sudden the sermons were transformed into dialogues. Now, the different issues brought up by the story were discussed together: did a woman need a dowry? Was the younger sister really condemned to a bad life after her calf was carried away? What does independence mean for a woman?

Further sessions continued to be successfully interactive. At the end of the cycle, many older people who could not read or who had trouble writing were helped by the younger students to fill out the final evaluation forms. Much was said in these comments about how young and old got to know each other better.

Did the process of gradual change between old and young do violence to the Latino notion of "respeto," of respect due to the older generation? Did the coordinator intrude with instructions on how the participants ought to relate to each other? Did we give out recipes on how Latino adolescents can adjust to North American society? I think not. The opportunity for a more open dialogue was made possible by the story itself: the word "piruja," prostitute, provided the spark, the complexities of the father-daughter relations opened avenues of communication, the poetic precocious wisdom of the boy gave courage to the young to speak up, and the astonishing, crude images of the flood carrying off bodies of cows with their hoofs sticking out of the torrent helped the old to hold off on ineffective moral platitudes. It was in Spanish, while discussing a work by a Latin American writer, that the members of this Latino intergenerational group found their own way to verbalize some of the difficulties that a new life in a North American city brought. Adjustments, behavior changes, and even reconsideration of moral edicts were debated in a public, democratic dialogue where complexities were recognized and solutions contemplated.

Overcoming barriers between communities

The intergenerational groups described above had been organized in Princeton and in Trenton respectively. I decided to test the possibility of mixing these two groups in order to see if adolescents and adults of two very different towns could engage each other in a true dialogue.

Friends who knew about the People and Stories/Gente y Cuentos Program in Trenton helped me make some further contacts with high school students and the director of the Princeton Senior Resource Center put me in touch with the director of the Office on Aging in the Department of Community Affairs in Trenton.

The plan was ambitious and demanding from the administrative point of view. The intergenerational format was to be kept but the composition of the groups would be complicated: older adults and high school students would be brought together but half would come from Princeton and half from Trenton. The meetings would alternate between Architects Housing, the Trenton facility for the aged, and the Princeton Senior Resource Center that had hosted our previous group. An English teacher in the Trenton high school became interested in the project and helped recruit the students. The older people were chosen from members of K-Plus Education in Aging Program, a group that tutored students in Trenton schools. The senior bus service was made available to transport both young and old from one town to another.

The first encounter was somewhat strained. The students from Trenton in their neat, best clothes—after all this was quite an occasion—eyed with astonishment the fashionable ragged blue jeans of the Princeton kids. No one knew what would happen next, but we, the organizers, were happy to see black and white, young, and old, with expectant faces waiting to begin.

Eudora Welty's[27] "A Worn Path" helped bring the group together or, to put it more accurately, start an unusually stormy discussion. In this classic story, Phoenix, an old, valiant black woman is performing a yearly pilgrimage from her distant rural home to the town's hospital to get the medicine her ailing grandson needs. She walks the long, long way muttering, giving herself courage to overcome the many obstacles, overgrown thorny paths, scary visions in lonely fields and a brutal encounter with a swaggering young hunter. Finally, at the hospital, she must answer the perfunctory inquiries of a questionnaire she hardly understands. While her wonderful assurance, her knowledge of proverbs and old sayings sustained her on her way and helped her overcome the violent encounter with the white hunter, at the

27   Eudora Welty. "A Worn Path." *A Curtain of Green*. New York: Modern Library, 1979.

hospital her want of know-how keeps her down, in the position of someone who lacks contemporary urban savvy. She could cope better with the emotional, ambiguous, seemingly friendly but really patronizing and aggressive speech of the hunter met on a country road than with the impersonal, technical questionnaire of the urban hospital authorities.

The story's vivid images helped launch the dialogue. Had anyone ever been afraid of black tree trunks at sundown that looked like menacing figures? Had anyone ever walked alone on such lonely rural paths? Had anyone ever had to face real danger in order to help another person?

The dramatic exchange between the young white hunter and the very old black woman started young and old on an exchange that dealt with lack of respect for women in general and for old women in particular. There was, however, a reluctance to speak directly about race and the reference to ethnicity finally came in a roundabout, quite unexpected way. At a certain point, a middle aged African American woman began very emotionally—she even stood up at one point—to criticize the story. "I am tired of all these stories where blacks speak like country bumpkins. My son makes seventy thousands dollars a year and we don't speak like that!" A silence followed; we had not anticipated such an outburst, such a critical and harsh judgment of a text which, up to then, had appeared as sensitive and beautiful. But soon another African American woman responded by saying that she thought that the black English used by the old woman was beautiful, that this musically accented speech was important to the black group, that it was related to a history that should not be forgotten. One of the white Princeton women mentioned that Eudora Welty was white — could she express the feelings of a black woman? Well, came the reply, plenty of authors write about subjects that are remote from them. Can we only talk about our own experience? But people kept coming back to the way Phoenix spoke. Were there persons today who talked as she did? If so, should they "reform" their speech and use only Standard English? What is proper language? For whom, when? The discussion after the participant's outburst was lively but remained rather tense. I felt worried. Would anyone come back next time? Everyone did.

In an evaluation at the end of the cycle, a white student from Princeton wrote: "The session on 'A Worn Path' was the most interesting one for me. I thought that Black English was a fact of life. I had no idea that it could mean such different things and that people felt so strongly about it."

Overcoming ethnic barriers

An English-as-a-Second-Language teacher in the Trenton High School helped organize a group in which African American and Latino students would discuss stories together. The teacher, a young, very well respected Chinese American woman, had been recommended to me by a Dominican staff person in the Department of Higher Education of the state of New Jersey as someone who had good contacts with the various groups in school. Indeed, she had no trouble recruiting sixteen students, all girls, eight Latinas and eight African Americans. She was able to obtain the agreement from the Principal to hold the sessions in the school building, immediately after the end of the afternoon classes.

As we began to plan the sessions, we decided to tailor the bibliography to the particular composition of this group. Half of the students spoke only English, yet we wished to introduce stories with both African American and Latino backgrounds. We chose three stories translated from the original Spanish; the other works would be by African American writers in English. We also looked for stories well rooted in their cultural milieu. We thought that each group would more readily react to voices that they immediately recognized as their own and that conversation between students who rarely talked to each other would start more easily on familiar themes explicitly anchored in a clearly recognizable tradition.

The dynamics turned out to be complex and we gradually understood that our wish to make things straightforward through our somewhat simplistic choice of stories had perhaps been a mistake.

When "The Fare" by the Puerto Rican writer José Luis Gonzalez[28] was read, the Latina students, as expected, started to talk first. Their immediate reactions to the coordinator's questions seemed more preoccupied with the African American students than with the text itself; they immediately set out to explain the story to the others, to the non Latinas.

In this story, a Puerto Rican man does not make it in New York; he becomes quite despondent and wants to return to his country but can't find anyone to lend him the money for the trip back. Did the African American students understand what it meant to be in another country in a moment of great need, isolated from one's family, with no one to turn to? The Puerto Rican students started telling the others stories about their own families, their Hispanic community. As I looked at them, they seemed to talk with one voice—the whole Latino group banded together, turned towards the African American group.

Conversely, the next time, when "Girl" by Jamaica Kincaid[29] was read, it was the African Americans who addressed the Latinas. In this three-page story a young girl reels off the spirited list

---

28   José Luis González. "El pasaje." *Todos los cuentos*. Méjico: UNAM, 1992.

29   Jamaica Kincaid. "Girl." *At the Bottom of the River*. New York: Vintage Books, 1985.

of her mother's admonitions, exacting, old-fashioned, but still revealing of the protective spirit of older black women towards their daughters. Here, the discussion took a somewhat different turn. The African American girls, again as a group, did a lot of explaining, mostly about black southern rural ways; but here the Puerto Ricans retorted that their families too were very strict. Both groups were surprised, as each had visualized the other as lax in its morals. The session became somewhat comical as each cluster tried to surpass the other in describing the strictness of their upbringing. "No, you just can't imagine how our family wants to control us!" "I must be in by eleven, even on Saturday night!" and so on. In this case a common problem was uncovered to the great astonishment of the participants. New information surfaced that brought the group together; they were after all teenagers having to deal with an older generation that did not understand them well.

While talking to each other, each group realized that they, unbeknownst to themselves, shared the prejudices of the society in which they lived. African American girls are mistakenly seen as generally more lax in their morals as others in school and the Latinas shared this point of view. The Latinas were suspected of being somehow more promiscuous, one of the many misconceptions about "Latin" culture that the African Americans shared with the majority, white "Anglo" population. Now, after discussing their families together, the students realized that they belonged to two groups that had a lot in common; for one thing, they were both seen by others as minorities with idiosyncratic ways. They also understood, perhaps only vaguely, that they themselves had been infected by the prejudices of the larger group. But, as the discussion of the story proceeded, they began opening up to each other and discovered, that as "minority" teenagers in Trenton, they shared some problems that could help them understand each other.

Was the choice of stories helpful after all? In a limited sense, yes. These stories caught the students' attention and made them want to talk, made them want to tell others about their own group. On the other hand, reading three Black and three Hispanic stories created a climate which almost forced the group to divide into two clear halves. The slow, individual first reactions to the story that surge from one's very own, private imagination and only gradually become more public during a meandering exchange could not happen in this setting. Each participant was almost forced into too quick an alignment with her own group (a constructed set of positions where certain opinions must prevail), and was pushed into telling the outsiders "how it really is" in the world of her own culture. While the process helped the students to break the silent distrust that usually reigns between them, it also prevented the discussion from experimenting with adventurous by-ways. The need to give others an understandable characterization promoted an overly clear, somewhat simplistic projection of a cultural identity profile that disregards individual differences and interesting variations.

The students enjoyed the sessions and talked about them later in their classes. The high school paper printed an article praising this unusual activity. However, mostly because of scheduling difficulties, we were unable to continue other People and Stories cycles in the Trenton High School. Nevertheless, the experience was important in pointing to certain challenges of multicultural programs.

The groups described above are only examples of programs that I organized in the early years. Eager to see what the reactions of different persons in a variety of circumstances would be, I continued to test the program with a number of very different participants. A "Port of Entry" program in a school involved adolescents recently arrived to the United States; an intergenerational program in a public library brought together students enrolled in a private school and older adults; a community college helped integrate sessions of Gente y Cuentos in a pre-GED program; several Catholic and Protestant churches opened their doors and encouraged their parishioners to join; African American parents who had organized their own, cooperative private school, participated and planned to adapt the approach to their own children.

At one point, a Hispanic organization in Arlington, Virginia, helped me to obtain a National Endowment for the Humanities (NEH) grant which allowed us to experiment with an even greater variety of programs in several states and in Puerto Rico. Very successful sessions were held with migrant workers in Florida and with very large mixed groups in Puerto Rico.

The invitation of CEDES, an Argentinean research organization, gave me the opportunity to have discussions with very poor groups of adults outside of Buenos Aires. People in the barrio Santa María were bent on improving their community. After building a church and a child care center, they expressed the desire to add a cultural program for adults. Gente y Cuentos was just right and I shall never forget the lively dialogues we had after reading short stories by Rulfo, García Márquez, Tizón, Asis and so many others, as we passed around little gourds of bitter matte.

UNDERSTANDING THE OTHER THROUGH LITERATURE

Diverse groups—older adults and adolescents, African American and Latino high school students, clients of different backgrounds of an urban Senior Daycare Center, citizens coming from suburbia and the inner city, immigrants from various Latin American and Caribbean countries—were all able to overcome initial difficulties in communication through their participation in People and Stories/Gente y Cuentos sessions. The program is successful even when the cleavages are deep.

The need for programs that will facilitate contacts between groups that feel estranged exists everywhere. Can People and Stories/Gente y Cuentos lessen this distrust of the other and encourage a willingness to listen with a more open mind?

We have seen how participants use their own experience during dialogues about short stories, how the questions of the coordinator help move the discussion from comments on the fictional text on the one hand to introspective, private references on the other, and how this may lead to a gradual opening to others in the group. But prejudice and fear may at times be so powerful that they block the access to a text that requires an active collaborative effort from its readers. How then can a discussion take place when the participants eye each other with distrust, or come to the first session with strong preconceived negative notions? How guarded will the dialogue remain in a group where persons may be fearful of revealing too much about themselves or of saying something that might not serve their own group well?

The power of literature, of the short story, is that it generates unexpected discussion topics that defy hackneyed responses. It establishes a playful mood, which encourages tinkering and experimentation, and its profusion of poetic details moves the imagination and steers it away from the beaten track. These aspects of fiction tend to engage people's creativity before resistance has a chance to set in. They produce an atmosphere where a mood of wonder and a desire to "find out" defeats the reluctance to move into new territory. These features of a text of fiction also require an intellectual effort, perhaps even a cooperative effort with unlikely companions. People are willing to engage in a truly searching dialogue about a short story while they are much more cautious and predictable during a programmed debate on more current issues.

Perhaps the best way to illustrate how works of fiction can create discussion and overcome barriers is to recall the details of some sessions.

"Encounter at Sundown" by the Uruguayan writer Eduardo Galeano,[30] is a story not entirely easy to make out at first. It is told in the voice of a young boy who has lost his beloved brother Mingo in an accident. The boy, in his refusal to accept Mingo's death, pretends that he can still play with him, that he can talk

---

30   Eduardo Galeano, "Secreto a la caída de la tarde." *Vagamundo.* Buenos Aires: Ediciones Crisis Libros, 1975.

to him. In his imagination, Mingo is still around, a wonderful, inventive playmate with whom he hunts birds, goes fishing, and explores the vast highland moors. Nevertheless, a fleeting consciousness of the reality brings the youngster close to a despair that pushes him to engage in dangerous, almost suicidal games. His parents consider him insane and submit him to the harshest of treatments, partly to punish him and partly to get the "devil" out of him. The boy too believes in a world of malevolent spirits and in the power of the evil eye and explains Mingo's death as having been caused by a set of magical circumstances. The story ends somewhat unexpectedly with dreamlike visions about a possible escape into a better world, toward an unknown sea.

Right at the start of the story, a fantastic reddish horse, with its flame-like mane brings Mingo to the rendezvous where his brother waits for him on the moor where the winds howl. Discussants never seem to object to the unreality of the scene, no one ever says that flying horses do not exist! Rather the compelling poetry with its powerful images, its mirror-like repetitions, its lulling rhythm, seems to open up the imagination for unexpected events. Besides, everyone has heard folk legends, and knows about fairy tale monsters and spectacular beasts. The very first lines of the text bring the readers to accept a different level of reality, a dreamlike world where anything may happen. At the same time, Galeano cleverly inserts incisive psychological details and indirect social commentaries: the boy cannot talk to anyone about the death of his brother in Pueblo Escondido (the Hidden Hamlet) so he shares his feelings only with his dog. He also does not dare to go to sleep: "I don't want to go to sleep. When I go to sleep I die."

Some questions of the coordinator can lead participants to begin to talk about their own reactions to the death of a loved one. The conversation starts close to the story. Were the parents right to forbid the boy to talk about his dead brother? Some think that the parents' cruelty is partly justified; they have so much work, they must survive, they can't dwell on the past, they must go on. Others differ. In Latin America the dead are with us forever and their pictures are often prominently displayed in the house. Most everyone has something to say and alternatives are proposed. Some stress the need to stick to conventions, to have commemorative ceremonies, while others bring up special cases and feel that sometimes a good psychiatrist could be helpful. Someone confesses that they too had problems with a death in their own family. Another participant mentions the imposed convention of silence about death in North American society and such a remark unites all those present and brings them to discuss what it means to adapt to a new culture.

The story's poetics enables some participants to say things here that conventional discourse would not tolerate, and they seem confident that it is permissible to go out on a limb, or to touch upon unusually difficult subjects. The story allows others in the group to do the same and slowly a climate of trust is established; no one needs to feel embarrassed. Still, when the boy explains that as far as he is concerned the truck ran over his brother because of an evil eye curse, participants often react cautiously. A sensitive chord is touched. Is it allowed to question rational explanations, reveal somewhat secret beliefs? Was the boy right in seeking occult explanations for a simple traffic accident? Does anyone ever do that? Almost invariably someone in the group will recount stories about incidents where the evil eye had a role to play and people hear each other out even on this delicate question. After all, the story talks about it, so why not also hear about other "more real" cases?

The coordinator brings participants back to the story and rereads the somewhat ambiguous passage where the boy seems to want to kill himself, when he dons the bearded Carnival mask of a devil with horns made of rags and races his bike down an embankment. "But it went badly and I fell safely on a garbage heap" says he rather comically. And then his parents hit him some more and dunk him in ice water. People laugh together at the line "it went badly and I fell safely" but soon the dialogue turns to the subject of how parents should treat their difficult children. Here very different opinions are voiced. In the story the "difficult" child is quite unusual. Is the boy really insane or has he found a way to resist an incredibly harsh world by retiring into dreams of his own where he can revel in the companionship of a beloved brother? Answers cannot be ready-made for the unusual questions raised by Galeano's short story. Participants help each other to understand the boy's character in depth by immersing themselves in the story, by drawing on their own experiences, by listening to what others have to say.

Finally, in the last paragraphs, the theme of the escape toward the sea is introduced. "Mingo told me that beyond the horizon I'll find the sea and that I was born to leave. To leave was I born." This powerful but ambiguous surge forward, out into the unknown, gets everyone to wonder. What does this mean? Where is he going? What sea? This passage provides a thrust toward some powerful, new, perhaps reckless, theme: how does one seek something better, how does one dare to leave, not knowing what's out there? Participants often end the session quietly, sharing reflections on their own migrations.

The story has generated difficult and sometimes most unusual questions that lead to an interaction where curiosity about the opinions of others forces people to hear each other out. In the end tolerance and understanding of the other result not because of some ethical admonition but because of the dynamics of the dialogue.

A second example, "A Worn Path" by Eudora Welty, which was read with youths and seniors of two different communities, can show how the scrutiny of striking poetic details can help participants to come together even though they may have started out with a certain amount of mutual distrust.

"A Worn Path" has images that produce strong dramatic tensions: silhouettes of trees that resemble "men with one arm," scarecrows that wave empty sleeves in the wind, fierce dogs that are ready to "sic," to attack. These powerful images almost compel participants to begin talking to each other. The rereading of the sentence "Big dead trees, like black men with one arm, were standing in the purple stalks of the withered cotton field" brought one African American participant to recall the lyrics of "Strange Fruit," the blues song about lynching that was made famous by Billie Holiday. But this sensitive subject was skirted by the group in the early stage of the discussion and several participants thought that those "big dead trees" meant only that the action was taking place during the winter months. The scarecrow figure was noticed and led some of the young white high school students to confess that they had seen scarecrows only in children's picture books; this brought some older African Americans from the South to share reminiscences about their rural past. Thus both young and old, regardless of their background, spoke more openly about fear—how fear can distort perception and how a simple straw puppet in a field can become a menacing figure ready to attack. Mention of danger and sudden assaults called attention to the unusual word "sic." No one seemed to understand its meaning until an older woman whose husband used to hunt, explained how the command orders dogs to pursue. Following her explanation, that terse, brutal word began to do its work and moved the discussion into a somewhat different direction. Questions were raised about the meaning of the whole episode about the encounter between the woman and the hunter with its constant shifts between the comic and the tragic. Everyone laughed at the scene in which, after tripping and falling into a bush of prickly weeds, Phoenix, the old woman, calls for help: "Lying on my back like a June-bug waiting to be turned over, mister." The mister is a white young hunter who suddenly appears out of nowhere, jokes with Phoenix a while, calling her "Granny," and finally lifts her out of the ditch. But soon the patronizing "Granny" turns into "you old colored people" as she continues to call him "Sir." This passage, these words, sparked a vigorous dialogue. Some younger people liked the old-fashioned term Granny; others, mostly older participants, felt that it was used here somewhat ironically to force the old woman back into helplessness. Young and old, black and white, discussed terms of address—kids, seniors, girls, Ma'am, Doctor, sweetie, etc. and how they might affect the characters in the story. The polite "Mister" and "Sir" used by Phoenix was contrasted with the condescending "Granny" of the hunter and brought everyone to talk about the escalation of the encounter. The hunter, still joking and laughing, suddenly points a gun at Phoenix. This unexpected and ambiguous turn of events jolted the group that did not quite know what to make of it. A question of the coordinator steered the participants to contrast this violent scene with another, very different encounter later in the story: as Phoenix finally arrives at her destination in the city where she hopes to collect again, as every year, the medicine that she needs for her sick grandson, a beautiful lady, smelling of roses, appears at her side and lovingly bends down to lace up her untied shoes. Some in the group wondered whether that kind lady was white or black, whether she was perhaps an angel, whether she was perhaps just a vision. Others picked up on that idea of a vision and began to speculate about the story as a whole. Was it only a dream? Had the grandson died a long time ago? Discussants became involved in various hypotheses as they began to search for the harder "facts" of the story. How old could Phoenix be? She says at one point "I never did go to school; I was too old at the Surrender." Who's Surrender? The participants tried to help each other estimate the possible age of the old woman while the coordinator assisted with facts of American history.

The last episode in the story, yet another encounter, this time with a hospital attendant, brought the discussion back to a more immediate present. As the old woman sits exhausted, finally having reached her destination, she must still fulfill certain requirements: "Speak up, Grandma...What's your name? We must have your history." That absurd "history" explodes here, and every participant in the group felt the shocking impact of this word. How far back do they want her to go? What sort of details will make up a history that will satisfy the attendant? So participants began talking about that word, about what "history" means here in the story as well as what it might mean for them personally. But they also talked about the woman's red kerchief, her long impractical skirts, her constant, colorful muttering, things that seemed to give a better idea of her history than any answers she might provide to the stilted questionnaire she needed to complete to become eligible for a "charity" case.

As people worked through the poetic landscape of the story, they were struck by a repetition, a contrast, a shadow, a stark image. So when suddenly, in the second part of the discussion, an older African American participant broke in to object to the way Blacks were made to speak by writers, it did not, fortunately, create a situation where participants would either retreat into an embarrassed silence or fall back on previously formulated frozen, antagonistic, either-or positions. The common, lively discussion that addressed so many of the story's poetic details had created a new climate where fresh arguments and different opinions were not only possible but seemed useful, interesting, and fun. Yes, there were tensions and plenty of disagreements on the subject of Black English, but in the end everyone was heard. Moreover, people realized that the work they had done together while discussing the poetics of the story had helped them unveil unsuspected facts about each other, and as we have already mentioned, a final evaluation rated "Worn Path" as particularly interesting and lively. Distrust of "the other" had broken down during the session.

THE ROAD TRAVELED

Looking back at the program after thirty five years, can we say that it is accomplishing its mission?

My original idea had been to share short stories that I enjoyed with persons who had never had access to literature. I felt that others than the educated had the right to partake of this pleasure. I also thought that talking together about these stories would give me an opportunity to be in touch in a more meaningful way with persons outside my immediate circle, that it would enlarge my own world. But as the program developed, it became apparent that much more was happening during these discussions of stories than I had anticipated.

When I heard a woman tell "It's hard for me to come, but I'll be here next week. This is the only thing I do for myself," I knew that those sessions were somehow extremely important for some of the participants, that those discussions touched their inner selves, helped them find what is important.

When I heard someone say "I've never thought I could talk so much just about stories," I realized that hearing one's own voice discussing the story's topics, poetic twists with others, can give a new self-assurance and becomes a living proof that one is capable to develop, defend, share opinions in a public forum.

When I heard someone say "I always thought that Black English was a fact of life but I see now that it means different things to different people," I understood that a fictitious literary story provides a safe, somewhat removed space where discussions of sensitive topics can take place.

When I heard young Hispanic adolescents say to seniors of the same community "You just don't know what it is to be in a Trenton high school" after reading a story by Juan Rulfo, I understood how a story could unlock inhibitions to allow communications between generations.

When I heard a woman say she found her own pearl, that she likes herself… "I'm changing. I am still looking for my own pearl. The story tells me there's hope that I'll find one," I understood how a story can connect to the life of the reader, and how it can give hope.

So with time, it becomes clear that People and Stories/Gente y Cuentos develops its own dynamic and ends up by doing much more than simply introduce a new public to literature. It seems that the intimate contact with fiction brings about a number of changes in the individual reader as well as between the members of a discussion group.

A successful discussion of a literary short story generates in the participants a good feeling; people seem strengthened by their participation in the dialogue, by hearing themselves express opinions and feelings on a variety of subjects. And it is that variety that a great short story introduces by offering a totally unexpected yarn. Both its themes and its language immerse readers in new worlds. Moreover, our method, where participants are helped to draw on their own life to enjoy and understand the intricacies of the story, encourages people to discover their own complexity and their own ability to reassess certain opinions, feelings, thoughts. At the same time, the dialogue which takes place with the other participants reveals a much greater diversity between the individuals sitting around the table than we had first imagined. Yes both Rosa and María are Latinas but they may not have the same ideas about how children should be educated. Not all African Americans view the use of Black English the same way; it might vary with their political views, their education, their taste in singing in church, their family connections, their profession. Mercedes in the very poor barrio outside of Buenos Aires was dreaming of ballet—yes, she was very poor but something in her craved for more beauty in her surroundings and the story that we were reading gave her the opportunity to identify and respect that craving and to share it with others who found her wish most surprising but recognized her right to have it.

This discovery of the unexpected both in others and in oneself at the contact of the story tends to do away with conventional labels. The story's characters, the often surprising twists of its narrative, its ambiguities, unusual images and language spark fresh perspectives which are interesting material for discussion with others. Works of fiction do not demand agreement or conclusions—there is no definite one way to react to a story but it is helpful to talk about our impressions with others. During these discussions, the usual simplistic categories which too often are used to pigeonhole people by their nationality, religion, gender, social status are exploded as the participants of the group exchange more intimate, more specifically individual opinions and preferences. The conversation oscillates between the participants and the story at hand; catchwords simply do not fit this interaction and are discarded as people search for more honest ways of expressing their own feelings and listen more attentively to what others have to say.

Thus group discussions about short stories not only lead to more tolerance; perhaps more importantly they lead to a richer, more intelligent discovery of oneself and of others. Difference is now perceived as strength rather than weakness. Each participant feels more conscious of her own make up, stronger, ready to be a more active and responsible member of a group where people are able to listen to each other and participate together in creating a more stimulating conversation. Possibly it is this discovery that a richer more perceptive life is possible that leads to a feeling of hope.

Could we say then, that participation in People and Stories/ Gente y Cuentos not only gives pleasure, improves critical abilities, increases self-assurance, but also helps participants to become stronger, more active and more discerning members of our civil society?

APPENDICES

ORGANIZATION

THEN AND NOW

When I started Gente y Cuentos in 1972 in Spanish, by myself, working as a volunteer with a group of Latino adults, I was far from imagining today's success.

People and Stories/Gente y Cuentos was incorporated as a Not For Profit Organization in 1993. It now involves a number of collaborators who develop programs in English, Spanish, and French in over fourteen US states, as well as in Latin America and France.

Patricia Andres is the present Executive Director. After taking part in the first 1987 training seminar, she became a most skillful coordinator and then co-director with me. In 1997 she was named Executive Director. The growth and vigor of today's program is in great part due to her gifted leadership.

Not For Profit Organization
Founder: Sarah Hirschman

Board of Directors:
    President
    Fourteen members

Executive Director:
    Development Consultant
    Managers of different programs (NEH, PACF, others)
    Additional staff as needed (remunerated, some volunteers)

Coordinators:

Using English, Spanish, French languages mostly remunerated but some work as volunteers

Funding:

Supported by Foundations as well as individual donors

Workshops:

All new coordinators attend two-day workshops given in Trenton, N.J. or in situ where intensive group practice takes place on how stories are examined and questions prepared. Basic background texts by Paulo Freire and Sarah Hirschman are discussed.

Office: People and Stories/Gente y Cuentos
140 East Hanover Street, Trenton, New Jersey, 08608
Phone: (609) 393-3230   FAX: (609) 989-8696
Web Site: www.peopleandstories.org

PROFILE OF GROUPS

In English: People and Stories
In Spanish: Gente y Cuentos
In French: Gens et Récits

Examples of groups that participated since 1972:

Urban Groups
Church parishioners
Senior citizens
Parents of African American cooperative school
Migrant women
Migrant workers
Newly arrived immigrants
Women in transition from welfare to work
Single mothers
Teen mothers
Adults in Argentinean barrio
Rural adults in South West France

Intergenerational groups
Inter-town intergenerational groups
Participants with different educational and social backgrounds
Groups of adults of various educational levels and from different social classes—Latino, and African American students

Learning centers
Public libraries in 14 states
Pre GED programs
Adult basic education
Disadvantaged students

Adults in nursing homes
Wounded soldiers, their doctors and caretakers (Bogotá, Colombia)
Handicapped adults
Residence and shelter for battered women
Homeless shelters
Troubled teenagers
Transitional housing facility
Homeless men recovering from drug abuse
Youth at risk (drugs, pregnancy)

Prisons
Youth on parole
Men recovering from substance abuse in early release from prison

EXAMPLES OF STORIES READ AND DISCUSSED

IN ENGLISH

Achebe, Chinua. "Marriage Is A Private Affair." 1952. *Girls at War and Other Stories*. New York: Fawcett, 1986.

Erdrich, Louise. "American Horse." *Braided Lives: An Anthology of Multicultural American Writing*, Ed. Minnesota Humanities Commission. St. Paul, MN: Minnesota Humanities Commission.

Hemingway, Ernest. "A Clean, Well-Lighted Place." 1927. *The Snows of Kilimanjaro*. New York: Charles Scribner's Sons, 1970, 1991.

Hughes, Langston. "Thank You, Ma'am." 1958. *Tales and Stories for Black Folks*. Ed. Toni Cade Bambara. Garden City: Zenith Books, 1971.

Malamud, Bernard. "The Model." 1983. *American Stories: Fiction from the Atlantic Monthly*. C. Michael Curtis, Ed. Chronicle Books: San Francisco, 1990.

McCullers, Carson. "A Tree, A Rock, A Cloud." *Collected Stories*. New York: Houghton Mifflin Co.1987.

IN SPANISH

Borges, Jorge Luis. "Emma Zunz." *El Aleph*. Buenos Aires, Argentina: Emecé Editores, 1957.

Gorodischer, Angélica. "La cámara oscura." *12 mujeres cuentan*. Buenos Aires, Argentina: Ed. La Campana, 1983.

Ribeyro, Julio Ramón. "La señorita Fabiola." *La palabra del mudo.* Lima, Perú: Milla Batres Editorial, 1972.

Rivera, Tomas. "La noche buena." *Y no se lo tragó la tierra.* Berkeley, California: Ed. Justa Publications, 1979.

Soto, Pedro Juan. "Garabatos." *Spiks.* Río Piedras, Puerto Rico: Editorial Cultural, 1970.

Valenzuela, Luisa. "Tango." *Simetrías.* Buenos Aires, Argentina: Editorial Sudamericana, 1993.

IN FRENCH

Adam, Olivier. « Cendres.» *Passer l'hiver.* Paris, France : Editions de l'Olivier (Seuil), 1998.

Chedid, Andrée. « L'Echarpe.» *La Femme en Rouge.* Paris, France, Flammarion, 2002.

Dhôtel, André. « L'Aigle dans la Ville.» *La nouvelle chronique fabuleuse.* Paris, France : Pierre Horay, 1984.

Kafka, Franz. « Un médecin de campagne.» *Dans la colonie pénitentiaire et autres nouvelles,* (traduit de l'allemand par Bernard Lortholary). Paris, France : Flammarion, 1991.

Maupassant, Guy de. « La parure.» *Contes du Jour et de la Nuit.* Paris, France :Folio, Gallimard, 1984.

Yourcenar, Marguerite. « Comment Wang-Fô fut sauvé.» *Nouvelles Orientales.* Paris, France: Gallimard, 1963.

Note: Short stories listed are approximately 10 pages long.

BIBLIOGRAPHY

WORKS THAT INFLUENCED THE DEVELOPMENT OF THE PEOPLE AND STORIES/GENTE Y CUENTOS PROJECT

Altamirano, Carlos y Sarlo, Beatriz. *Literatura/Sociedad*. Buenos Aires: Libreria Hachette, 1983.

Alter, Robert. *The Art of Biblical Narrative*. New York: Basic Books, 1981.

_____ *The Pleasures of Reading in an Ideological Age*. New York: Simon and Schuster, 1989.

Arasse, Daniel. *Le Détail*. Paris: Flammarion, 1992.

Bakhtin, Mikhail M. *Problemy tvorchestva Dostoevskogo*. Leningrad: Priboi, 1929. In English: *Problems of Dostoevsky's Poetics*. Minneapolis: University of Minnesota Press, 1984.

_____ *Tvorchestvo Fransua Rable*. Moscow: Khudozhest-vennaia literatura, 1965. In English: *Rabelais and His World*. Trans. Helene Iswolsky. Cambridge, MA: MIT Press, 1968.

_____ *Voprosy literatury i estetiki.* Moscow: Khudozhest-
vennaia literatura, 1975. In English:four essays in *The Dialogic
Imagination.* Trans. Caryl Emerson and Michael Holquist. Austin:
University of Texas Press, 1981.

Barthes, Roland. *Le Plaisir du texte.* Paris: Seuil, 1973. In English:
The Pleasure of the Text. Trans. Richard Miller. New York: Hill and
Wang, 1975.

_____ *Le Degré zero de l'écriture.* Paris: Seuil, 1953. In
English: *Writing Degree Zero.* Trans. Annette Lavers and Colin
Smith: New York: Hill and Wang, 1978.

Benjamin, Walter. *Illuminations.* New York: Harcourt Brace Jovanovich,
1969.

_____ *Reflections.* New York: Harcourt Brace Jovanovich, 1978.

Berger, John. *Ways of Seeing.* Harmondsworth, Middlesex, England:
Penguin Books, 1972.

Bleich, David. *The Double Perspective: Language, Literacy and Society.*
New York: Oxford University Press, 1988.

Bourdieu, Pierre. *Esquisse d'une théorie de la pratique. Précédée de trois
études d'éthnologie kabyle.* Genève: Droz, 1972.

Burke, Kenneth. *A Rhetoric of Motives.* New York: Prentice-Hall,
1950.

_____ *Language as Symbolic Action.* Berkeley: University of
California Press, 1966.

Calvino, Italo. *Six Memos for the Next Millennium.* Cambridge, MA:
Harvard Univ. Press, 1988.

Candido, Antonio. *Literatura e Sociedade*. São Paulo: Companhia Editora Nacional, 1965.

_____ *No sala de aula*. São Paulo: Editora Atica, 1986.

Certeau, Michel de. *L'Invention du quotidien. 1. Arts de faire*. Paris: Editions Gallimard, 1990. In English: *The Practice of Everyday Life*. Trans. Steven F. Rendall. Berkeley: University of California Press, 1984.

Clifford, James. *The Predicament of Culture: Twentieth-Century Ethnography, Literature and Art*. Cambridge, MA: Harvard University Press, 1988.

Cobo Borda, J.G. *La alegria de leer*. Bogotá: Instituto Colombiano de Cultura, 1976.

Coleridge, Samuel Taylor. "Occasion of the Lyrical Ballads." In *Biographia Literaria*, Ch. XIV. London: Dent, 1956 (1817).

Coles, Robert. *The Call of Stories: Teaching and the Moral Imagination*. Boston: Houghton Mifflin, 1989.

Compagnon, Antoine. *La Troisième république des lettres: de Flaubert à Proust*. Paris: Seuil, 1983.

Cortázar, Julio. *Rayuela*. Buenos Aires: Editorial Sudamericana, 1963. In English: *Hopscotch*. Trans. Gregory Rabassa. New York: Pantheon, 1966.

Cows, Mary Ann. *The Eye in the Text*. Princeton: Princeton University Press, 1981.

Culler, Jonathan. "Beyond Interpretation: The Prospects of Contemporary Criticism." *Comparative Literature 28* (1978), pp. 244-56.

Dewey, John. *Art as Experience.* New York: G.P. Putnam's Sons, 1934.

Diderot, Denis. *Jacques le fataliste et son maitre.* Paris: Bibliothèque de la Pléiade, NRF, 1935(1773). In English: *Jacques the Fatalist and his Master.* Trans. Wesley D. Camp and Agnes G. Raymond, New York: P. Lang, 1984.

Dilthey, W. *Poetry and Experience.* Princeton: Princeton University Press, 1985.

Dorfman, Ariel. *Hacia la liberación del lector Latinoamericano.* Hanover: Edic. del Norte, 1984.

Eikhenbaum, Boris Mikhailovich. *Literatura.* Leningrad, 1927.

Empson, William. *Seven Types of Ambiguity.* New York: New Directions Publishing Corporation, 1966 (1930).

Fanger, Donald. *The Creation of Nikolai Gogol.* Cambridge: Harvard University Press, 1979.

Fish, Stanley. *Is there a Text in this Class? The Authority of Interpretive Communities.* Cambridge, MA: Harvard University Press, 1980.

Fisher, Philip. *Hard Facts: Setting and Form in the American Novel.* New York: Oxford University Press, 1985.

Franco, Jean. *An Introduction to Spanish American Literature.* London: Cambridge University Press, 1969.

Freire, Paulo. *Educação como pratica da liberdade.* Rio de Janeiro: Paz e Terra, 1967. In English: *Cultural Action for Freedom.* Cambridge MA: Harvard Educational Review, 1970. (Monogaph series no.1).

_____ *Pedagogia del Oprimido*. Montevideo, Uruguay: Tierra Nueva, 1970. In English: *Pedagogy of the Oppressed*. Trans. Myra Bergman Ramos. New York: Herder and Herder, 1970.

Frye, Northrop. *Anatomy of Criticism*. Princeton: Princeton University Press, 1957.

Fuentes, Carlos. *La nueva novela hispanoamericana*. México: Joaquín Mortiz, 1969.

_____ *Casa con dos puertas*. México: Joaquín Mortiz, 1970.

Gadamer, Hans Georg. *Wahrheit and Methode*. Tubingen: J.C.B. Mohr, 1960. In English: *Truth and Method*. Trans. Garrett Barden and John Cumming, New York: Crossroad Publishing Co., 1984.

García Márquez, Gabriel. *Cien años de soledad*. Buenos Aires: Sudamericana, 1967. In English: *One Hundred Years of Solitude*. Trans. Gregory Rabassa, New York: Harper, 1970.

Gaventa, John. *Power and Powerlessness*. Urbana: University of Illinois Press, 1980.

Geertz, Clifford. *Local Knowledge*. New York: Basic Books, 1983.

Genette, Gérard. *Figures III*. Paris: Seuil, 1972. In English: *Figures, vol. 1-3*. Trans. Alan Sheridan. New York: Columbia University Press, 1982.

Goffman, Erving. *Frame Analysis*. New York: Harper & Row, 1974.

Gombrich, E.H. *Art and Illusion*. New York: Pantheon Books, 1960.

Goodman, Nelson. *Of Mind and Other Matters*. Cambridge: Harvard University Press, 1984.

Greenblatt, Stephen. *Renaissance Self-Fashioning*. Chicago: University of Chicago Press, 1980.

Greenblatt, Stephen and Gunn, Giles, ed. *Redrawing the Boundaries*. New York: MLA, 1992.

Harss, Luis and Dohmann, Barbara. *Into the Mainstream*. New York: Harper & Row, 1967.

Hirschman, Albert O. *A Bias For Hope*. New Haven: Yale University Press, 1971.

_____ *Getting Ahead Collectively*. New York: Pergamon Press, 1984.

_____ *Rival Views of Market Society*. New York: Viking, 1986.

Holland, Norman N. *The Dynamics of Literary Response*. New York: Oxford University Press, 1968.

Iser, Wolfgang. *The Act of Reading: A Theory of Aesthetic Response*. Baltimore: Johns Hopkins University Press, 1978.

_____ *Prospecting: From Reader Response to Literary Anthropology*. Baltimore: The John Hopkins University Press, 1989.

_____ *The Implied Reader: Patterns of Communication in Prose Fiction from Bunyan to Beckett*. Baltimore: Johns Hopkins University Press, 1978.

Jakobson, Roman. "Closing Statement: Linguistic and Poetics." *Style in Language*. Ed.T.A. Sebeok. Cambridge MA: M.I.T. Press, 1960.

Jameson, Frederic. *The Prison-House of Language*. Princeton: Princeton University Press, 1972.

Jauss, Hans Robert. *Aesthetic Experience and Literary Hermeneutics.* Trans. Michael Shaw. Minneapolis: University of Minnesota Press, 1982.

Kantor, Tadeusz. *Le Théâtre de la mort.* Lausanne: Editions L'Age d' homme, 1970.

Koch, Kenneth. *Rose, Where Did You Get That Red?* New York: Random House, 1973

Kundera, Milan. *L'Art du roman.* Paris: Gallimard, 1986. In English: *The Art of the Novel.* Trans. Linda Asher. New York: Grove Press, 1988.

Labov, William. *Language in the Inner City.* Philadelphia: University of Pennsylvania Press, 1972.

Leenhardt, Jacques. *Lecture politique du roman.* Paris: Editions de Minuit, 1973.

Lévi-Strauss, Claude. *La Pensée sauvage.* Paris: Librairie Plon, 1962. In English: *The Savage Mind.* Chicago: University of Chicago Press, 1966.

_____ *Tristes tropiques.* Paris: Plon, 1958. In English: *Tristes Tropiques.* trans. J. Russell. New York: Criterion, 1962.

Liebow, Elliot. *Tally's Corner.* Boston: Little, Brown and Co., 1967.

Lotman, Jurij. *Struktura khudozhestvennogo teksta.* Moskva: "Iskustvo", 1970. In English: *The Structure of the Artistic Text.* Trans. Ronald Vroon. Ann Arbor: Dept. of Slavic Languages and Literature, 1977.

Morrison, Toni. "Unspeakable Things Unspoken: The Afro-American Presence in American Literature." *Michigan Quarterly Review*, Winter 1989, pp.1-34, Michigan: University of Michigan.

Mullaney, Steven. "Playing on the margins: the social and cultural situation of the English Renaissance stage." *The Cambridge History of Literary Criticism*, Vol.3, ed. Glyn P. Norton. Cambridge: Cambridge University Press, 1995.

Noam, Gil. G. "Beyond Freud and Piaget: Biographical Worlds-Interpersonal Self." *Morality and Personal Development*, pp. 360-398.

Ong, Walter J. *Orality and Literacy*. New York: Methuen, 1982.

Ortega, Julio. *La contemplación y la fiesta*. Caracas: Monte Avila Editores, 1969.

Patte, Geneviève. *Laissez-les lire!* Paris: Les Editions ouvrières et Pierre Zech editeur, 1978.

Perez, Jr. Louis A. *Essays on Cuban History*. Gainesville, FL: University of Florida, 1995.

Pratt, Mary Louise. *Toward a Speech Act - Theory of Literary Discourse*. Bloomington: Indiana Press, 1977.

Pratt, Mary Louise and Traugott, Elizabeth Close. *Linguistics for Students of Literature*. New York: Harcourt Brace Jovanovich, 1980.

Propp, Vladimir. *Morfologija skazki*. Leningrad, 1928. In English: *Morphology of the Folktale*. Trans. L. Scott Austin: University of Texas Press, 1968.

Putnam, Robert D. "The Prosperous Community - Social Capital and Public Life." *The American Prospect*. (Spring 1993), pp. 35-42.

Richards, I.A. *Practical Criticism.* New York: Harcourt, Brace & World, Inc., 1929.

Ricoeur, Paul. *Histoire et vérité.* Paris: Editions du Seuil, 1955. In English: *History and Truth.* Trans. Charles A. Kelbey. Evanston, IL: Northwestern University Press, 1965.

_____ *La Métaphore vive.* Paris: Seuil, 1975. In English: *The Rule of Metaphor.* Trans. Robert Czerny, Toronto: Univ. of Toronto Press, 1977.

Riffaterre, Michael. *La Production du texte.* Paris: Editions du Seuil, 1979. In English: *Text Production.* Trans. Térèse Lyons. New York: Columbia University, 1983.

Rorty, Richard. *Philosophy and the Mirror of Nature.* Princeton: Princeton University Press, 1979.

_____ *Essays on Heidegger and Others.* (Philosophical Papers, vol. 2). Cambridge; New York: Cambridge University Press, 1991.

Rosenblatt, Louise M. *The Reader, the Text, the Poem: The Transactional Theory of the Literary Work.* Carbondale, IL: Southern Illinois Univ. Press, 1978.

_____ *Literature as Exploration.* New York: MLA, 1995 (First Edition 1938).

Sartre, Jean-Paul. "Qu'est-ce que la littérature?" *Situations II.* Paris: Gallimard, 1948. In English: *What Is Literature? And Other Essays.* Cambridge: Harvard University Press, 1988.

Scholes, Robert. *Textual Power.* New Haven: Yale University Press, 1985.

Schwarz, Roberto. *Misplaced Ideas.* London: Verso, 1992.

_____ *Qué horas são?* São Paulo: Editora Schwarcz Ltda., 1987.

Shklovskij, Viktor. "Tristram Shandy." *Texte der Russischen Formalisten,* (Band 1), München, 1969.

Shor, Ira. *Empowering Education: Critical Teaching for Social Change.* Chicago: University of Chicago Press, 1992.

Sommers, Joseph. *After the Storm, Landmarks of the Modern Mexican Novel.* University of New Mexico Press, 1968.

Stevick, Earl W. *Teaching Languages - A Way and Ways.* Rowley, MA: Newbury House, 1980.

Suleiman, Susan R. *The Reader in the Text.* Princeton, NJ: Princeton Univ. Press, 1980.

Tompkins, Jane P. ed. *Reader-Response Criticism.* Baltimore: The Johns Hopkins University Press, 1980.

Vargas Llosa, Mario. *La casa verde.* Barcelona: Seix Barral, 1965. In English: *The Green House.* Trans. Gregory Rabassa. New York: Harper & Row, 1968.

_____ *García Márquez: Historia de un deicidio.* Barcelona: Barral Editores, 1971.

Vygotsky, Lev Semenovich. *Mind in Society.* Cambridge MA: Harvard Univ. Press, 1978(1962).

_____ *Thought and Language.* Cambridge, MA: MIT Press, 1986.

Walzer, Michael. *Spheres of Justice: a Defense of Pluralism and Equality.* New York: Basic Books, 1983.

_____ *What It Means To Be An American.* New York: Marsilio, 1992.

West, Cornel. *Race Matters.* New York: Vintage Books, 1994.

White, Michael. "Deconstruction and Therapy." *Therapeutic Conversations.* New York: W.W. Norton, 1993. Also in the same volume: Jill Freedman and Gene Combs "Invitations to new stories: Using questions to explore alternative possibilities."

SHORT STORIES CITED

<u>In Spanish and English</u>

García Márquez, Gabriel. "La siesta del martes." *Los funerales de la Mamá Grande.* Xalapa, México: Universidad Veracruzana, 1962.

_____ "Tuesday Siesta." *No One Writes to the Colonel and Other Stories.* Trans. from Spanish. New York: Harper&Row, 1968.

González, José Luis. "En el fondo del caño hay un negrito." *Cuentos puertorriqueños de hoy.* Río Piedras, Puerto Rico: Editorial Cultural, 1985.

_____ "There is a little black boy in the ditch." *Cuentos*, ed. Karl Wagenheim. New York: Schocken Books, 1978.

Rulfo, Juan. "Es que somos muy pobres." *El llano en llamas y otros cuentos.* México: Fondo de Cultura Económica, 1955.

_____ "But we are very poor." *Burning Plain and Other Stories.* Transl. G.D. Shade. Austin: University of Texas Press, 1967.

<u>In Spanish</u>

Arguedas, Jose María. "Hijo solo." *Amor mundo y todos los cuentos.* Lima, Perú: Ed. Francisco Moncloa, 1967.

Moyano, Daniel. "Artistas de variedades." *"La espera" y otros cuentos.* Buenos Aires, Argentina: Centro Editor de América Latina, 1982.

Galeano, Eduardo. "Secreto a la caída de la tarde." *Vagamundo.* Buenos Aires: Crisis Libros, 1975.

Rey Rosa, Rodrigo. "La prueba." *El cuchillo del mendigo/El agua quieta.* Barcelona: Seix Barral, 1992.

Tizón, Hector. "Petróleo." *El jactancioso y la bella.* Buenos Aires, Argentina: Centro Editor de América Latina, 1972.

In English

Kincaid, Jamaica. "Girl." *At the Bottom of the River.* New York: Vintage Books, 1985.

Updike, John. "Dear Alexandros." *Pigeon Feathers.* New York: Alfred A. Knopf, 1962.

Walker, Alice. "Everyday Use." *In Love and Trouble.* New York: Harcourt, Brace, Jovanovich, 1973.

Welty, Eudora. "A Worn Path." *A Curtain of Green.* New York: Modern Library, 1979.

In French and English

Mahfouz, Naguib. "A la recherche de Zaabalâwi." *L'Amour au pied des pyramides.* (traduit de l'arabe par Richard Jacquemond), Paris : Babel, 2002.

_____ "Searching for Zaabalawi." *The Time and the Place, and other Stories.* Doubleday, 1991. - Anchor, Reprint edition, 2001.